Corporate Social Responsibility: A Very Short Introduction

VERY SHORT INTRODUCTIONS are for anyone wanting a stimulating and accessible way in to a new subject. They are written by experts, and have been translated into more than 40 different languages.

The Series began in 1995, and now covers a wide variety of topics in every discipline. The VSI library now contains over 350 volumes—a Very Short Introduction to everything from Psychology and Philosophy of Science to American History and Relativity—and continues to grow in every subject area.

Very Short Introductions available now:

Available soon:

For more information visit our website

www.oup.com/vsi/

Jeremy Moon

CORPORATE SOCIAL RESPONSIBILITY

A Very Short Introduction

OXFORD
UNIVERSITY PRESS

Great Clarendon Street, Oxford, OX2 6DP,
United Kingdom

Oxford University Press is a department of the University of Oxford.
It furthers the University's objective of excellence in research, scholarship,
and education by publishing worldwide. Oxford is a registered trade mark of
Oxford University Press in the UK and in certain other countries

First edition published in 2014

Impression: 6

Published in the United States of America by Oxford University Press
198 Madison Avenue, New York, NY 10016, United States of America

British Library Cataloguing in Publication Data

Data available

Library of Congress Control Number: 2014945169

ISBN 978-0-19-967181-6

Printed in Great Britain by
Ashford Colour Press Ltd., Gosport, Hampshire.

This book is dedicated to all the staff, students, and visitors of the International Centre for Corporate Social Responsibility, University of Nottingham, with whom I have learned so much.

It is also dedicated to my friend Louis Warren and all those that do Corporate Social Responsibility, without whom it would only be an idea.

Contents

Contents

Acknowledgements

I have learned so much about Corporate Social Responsibility (CSR) from the staff, students, and academic visitors of the International Centre for Corporate Social Responsibility, University of Nottingham. Many of these also helped me with specific questions I had in preparing the manuscript.

More broadly, I thank all the contributors to the academic field of CSR, whose papers I am unable to reference in this book. They have built the body of work on which this *Very Short Introduction* draws.

Over the thirty years in which I have studied CSR, I have learned so much from people practising it, particularly in the UK, Australia, the USA, Canada, India, Singapore, and China. This learning has been through formal interviews; informal chats in coffees shops or pubs; and observation of CSR professionals in meeting rooms, factories, mining communities, fishing villages, or remote desert locations.

I am grateful to the academic institutions in which I have worked whilst writing this book. Most of the writing took place during a period of study leave from the University of Nottingham when I was also the Gourlay Professor of Ethics in Business, Trinity College, University of Melbourne. The manuscript was finalized in my new position as Velux Professor of Corporate Sustainability, Copenhagen Business School.

I am grateful for the encouragement and support of OUP staff, David Musson, Andrea Keegan, Jenny Nugee, Emma Ma, and an anonymous editorial reader, to the anonymous external reviewers of my proposal, and to Tom Chandler the copy editor.

Finally, the manuscript has benefited immensely from those who read the final draft: Michael Humphreys, Dirk Matten, Andrew Pilkington, and Andreas Rasche.

List of abbreviations

AACSB	Association to Advance Collegiate Schools of Business
AMBA	Association of MBAs (Masters of Business Administration)
ASEAN	Association for South East Asian Nations
BITC	Business in the Community
CSR	Corporate Social Responsibility
EQUIS	European Quality Improvement System
ESG	Environmental, Social and Governance (reporting requirements)
ETI	Ethical Trade Initiative
EITI	Extractive Industries Transparency International
FTSE4Good	Financial Times Stock Exchange 4 Good
GRI	Global Reporting Initiative
ILO	International Labor Organization
ISO	International Standards Organization
LDCs	Least developed countries
MNCs	Multinational Corporations
SA8000	Social Accountability 8000
SMEs	Small and Medium-sized Enterprises
SOEs	State Owned Enterprises
SRI	Socially Responsible Investment
UNGC	United Nations Global Compact
UNICEF	United Nations Children's Fund
UNPRI	United Nations Principles for Responsible Investment
UNPRME	United Nations Principles for Management Education

List of boxes

Introduction

I have never known much good done by those who affected to trade for the public good.

Adam Smith, moral philosopher
and a pioneer of political economy (1776)

Corporate Social Responsibility (CSR) has been described as 'an oxymoron' by all too many dinner party pundits who are suspicious of business claims about its sociability. They point to a compendium of cases of corporate irresponsibility, from Union Carbide's Bhopal explosion to the Enron fraud; from Siemens' corruption to BP's Deepwater Horizon disaster; from adverse business impacts upon climate change to financial sector irresponsibility; and all too many more.

CSR has also been described as 'a fundamentally subversive doctrine' by Nobel Prize-winning economist, Milton Friedman, the most prominent modern standard-bearer for Adam Smith. Friedman and his acolytes worry about CSR distracting from the prime social purpose of business as they see it: maximizing profits for the company shareholders. It is through profit-making, they argue, that business provides core social contributions of employment and taxation, and expeditiously meets customer demands for goods and services.

Friedman, like former US Secretary of Labor, Robert Reich, and countless others on the left of politics, also sees CSR as intruding upon, or occluding, the proper responsibility of government.

In the face of such apparent unanimity about the dangers of CSR, one might wonder why CSR is worthy even of a *Very Short Introduction*. I intend to demonstrate that CSR is increasingly central to our understanding of business–society relationships.

Chapter 1
An idea whose time has come

CSR is an idea whose time has come
> Martin Wolf, Chief Economics Commentator,
> *Financial Times* (2002)

But what is CSR?

At its core, CSR concerns the ways in which companies manage their relations with society. Pioneering CSR scholar, Howard Bowen, defined it as 'obligations...to pursue those policies, to make those decisions, or follow those actions which are desirable in terms of the objectives and values of our society'.

Box 1 illustrates the development of definitions. Davis's definition focuses on the non-core elements of the business, whereas Carroll assumes that the responsibility is for all facets of the company. Matten and Moon emphasize that CSR is for societal good, and note the key role of the corporation in interpreting societal expectations and selecting its policies.

> ## Box 1 Definitions of CSR
>
> 'the firm's consideration of, and response to, issues beyond the narrow economic, technical, and legal requirements of the firm' (Keith Davis, 1973)
>
> 'the economic, legal, ethical and discretionary expectations that society has of organizations' (Archie Carroll, 1979)
>
> 'policies and practices of corporations that reflect business responsibility for some of the wider societal good. Yet the precise manifestation and direction of the responsibility lie at the discretion of the corporation' (Dirk Matten and Jeremy Moon, 2008)

Numerous definitions of CSR are offered by academics and commentators, and by business, civil society, governmental and consulting organizations. Overall, the definitions capture the following key features:

- business responsibility *to* society (i.e. being accountable)
- business responsibility *for* society (i.e. in compensating for negative impacts and contributing to societal welfare);
- business responsible *conduct* (i.e. the business needs to be operated ethically, responsibly, and sustainably);
- business responsibility to and for society in broad terms (i.e. including environmental issues); and
- the management by business of its relationships with society.

Nevertheless, CSR can be difficult to pin down. It is simultaneously an idea or set of societal expectations; and a set of business practices. Its underlying ideas and contemporary practices are contextual, particularly reflecting its company, sectoral, national, ethnic, and cultural location. It overlaps with a number of other concepts, such as ethics, sustainability, and citizenship. Its meanings, assumptions, and implications for business and society have been dynamic. Hence definitions of CSR are not only plentiful but also continually emerging.

Who is involved in CSR?

Although one of the reasons for the emergence of CSR concerns the distinctive power of the corporate organizational form, the CSR ethos and its practices have been embraced by all sorts of businesses. Thus, not only national corporations and multinational corporations (MNCs), but also a wider range of businesses (e.g. small and medium-sized enterprises (SMEs), state-owned enterprises (SOEs)) also claim to practise CSR. Notwithstanding, the company being the critical CSR organization, a key feature of contemporary CSR is that it is taken seriously, engaged in, and promoted by a much wider set of organizations including labour, finance, governmental, civil society, and professional organizations (Box 2).

> ### Box 2 Organizations adopting or engaging with CSR
>
> *Business* national corporations; MNCs; SMEs; SOEs; family-owned businesses; business associations (e.g. Institute of Directors, Chambers of Commerce)
>
> *Labour* national trade unions; international trade union organizations (e.g. ILO; International Trade Union Confederation, IndustriALL Global Union, the International Union of Food Workers)
>
> *Finance* national stock exchanges; Dow Jones Index, FTSE Index

The involvement of the wider range of organizations in CSR
reflects both their interest in the social impacts of business and
their view that CSR is a means of addressing a wider set of societal
concerns, such as labour standards, human rights, and climate
change. These non-business organizations have become involved
in CSR through a variety of roles, such as being involved in CSR
standard setting, collaborating with companies' CSR policies, and
auditing and evaluating company CSR performance. As a result,
CSR now features in a growing set of networks and organizations
which institutionalize business behaviours and relate these to
societal challenges.

Unpacking CSR

The clue to CSR is in the name!

The *C* in CSR refers to policies, practices, and impacts of
corporations. There are special reasons for expecting *corporations*,
as opposed to other businesses, to be socially responsible.
Historically this was by virtue of the special licences that
corporations were granted by governments to pursue large public

projects like canal or road building. Subsequently, this was because of the limited liability status granted to corporations which meant that society needed additional assurance about their sociability. More recently, the sheer size of corporate social impacts (e.g. through employment, provision of public utilities and critical infrastructure, global supply chains, the consequences of the financial crisis) has justified special attention to CSR.

The concept of CSR extends beyond corporations alone to include businesses more generally. (Some public agencies and universities also assume CSR but this is outside our purview). Indeed, the concepts of business philanthropy, paternalism, and stewardship pre-date the rise of the modern corporation and originally reflected the responsibilities taken by individual business owners.

The *S* in CSR captures the location, dependence upon, and responsibility of business to society. Businesses employ, sell to, and are owned by members of society. This suggests that socially egregious behaviour risks social punishment through, for example, boycotts or targeted action or social media critique. It also suggests that there may be rewards for companies that meet and even exceed broad societal expectations. The S is usually taken to include environmental responsibility, reflecting CSR's broadly anthropomorphic assumptions about the environment.

The *R* in CSR signals the assumption of an obligation to be accountable or liable for something. In other words, CSR signals that companies take responsibility for, and are answerable for, their actions and impacts. Systems of accountability usually rest on such ethical concepts as stewardship and trust, or more sociological and political concepts such as reciprocity, social contracts, and citizenship. Accountability in CSR is now associated with formal reporting of social and environmental actions and impacts, either within general company reports or through dedicated CSR reports.

Beyond these basic elements, CSR dynamics reflect changing ethical mores of business leaders and corporate cultures; new issues for which society holds business responsible; new opportunities which businesses identify to attract customers, investors, or employees; and changing assumptions about management among consultants and business schools. The dynamics vary as a result of the particular stress put on points of overlap of CSR with, for example, ethics, governance, citizenship, and sustainability. They also vary by context, particularly the expectations of business responsibility embedded in national business systems.

The antecedents of CSR

There are ethical antecedents to CSR embodied in ancient Persian, Jewish, Hindu, Christian, Confucian, and Islamic texts and social conventions which point to particular obligations of individuals who are well endowed. These included treating others fairly, supporting the needy, and being good stewards of the resources with which one had been blessed. These morés have been drawn upon, adopted and adapted in modern manifestations of business responsibility.

More specific ethical antecedents of CSR relating to social expectations of, and self-descriptions by, business people have also been around for centuries. In European traditions these are often defined in terms of philanthropy ('love of humanity') and paternalism (a 'fatherly'—though we might today say 'parental'—attitude of care and protection to dependants).

The concept of philanthropy is perhaps the most ubiquitous antecedent of modern CSR. Most managerial and academic understandings of CSR include reference to philanthropic contributions in support of charitable causes. This was evident on the part of individual business owners in the 19th century and in the creation of foundations of those who have acquired vast personal wealth through corporations from Andrew Carnegie and John

D. Rockefeller to Bill Gates. It is also evident in the establishment of corporate foundations, such as the Ford, Leverhulme, Novo Nordisk, Nuffield, Shell, Tata, or Velux foundations. Historically, corporate philanthropy was associated with: relief of poverty; alleviation of disease; and the advance of education, science, and the arts.

Another element of the CSR genealogy is industrial paternalism. This was a feature of 19th century industrialization manifest in the provision of housing, education and recreational facilities, and opportunities for workers. In some cases this was in purpose-built communities like Cadbury's 'Bourneville' village and the Lever Brothers' 'Port Sunlight' 'in the UK'. However, industrial paternalism was more usually embedded in existing communities. Thus retail pharmacist, Boots, created and ran schools in Nottingham, England before governmental provision. Contemporary forms of industrial paternalism include social provision for employees and families in mining complexes in remote parts of Australia, Canada, Nigeria, and Zambia, for example.

Recent developments

Since the 1990s, CSR has given greater emphasis to the social impacts of business operations themselves, including not only practices in companies' own operations , such as health and safety, diversity and equal opportunities policies, and consumption of scarce resources, but also those occurring in international supply chains, for example labour conditions in developing countries' agriculture, textile, and footwear industries. Such an emphasis also includes the way products and services are used and disposed of, and may generate policies on packaging and recycling, responsible consumption of alcohol, and children's food and drink products. Some companies select and market products and services precisely for their social responsibility criteria—fair trade or ethically sourced products, for example—in the expectation that this will meet consumer preferences; some, like Italian fashion company Benetton, have used the language of sustainability and sustainable development to indicate how their CSR is aligned with broader societal agendas.

In the last decade or so, there has been attention not just to the direct impacts of business as a focus for company responsibility, but also to the broader social, environmental, and economic conditions within which business can prosper. In this light, companies have taken up various areas of responsibility: addressing diseases in Africa (e.g. German logistics company DHL and AIDS in Africa); the general availability of natural resources (e.g. Unilever and Coca Cola and water); and the health of the economy (e.g. members of the UK Business in the Community encourage entrepreneurship and training). Whilst in some cases these themes can be likened to the agendas of philanthropy and paternalism, they can also entail much greater closeness to the activities of charities, non-governmental organizations (NGOs), and governments. Thus, some companies have applied the term 'corporate citizenship' to capture these more political manifestations of CSR.

This summary of recent trends illustrates that CSR is very much bound up in the more general observation about CSR being, contextual, overlapping, and dynamic. Critically, the dynamics of CSR do not just happen. They tend to reflect societal contestation about, and legitimation of, the issues for which companies are held responsible by society; the justifications for the responsibilities which businesses espouse; and the strategies taken to manifest these responsibilities.

From the margins to the mainstream

Outside the USA, and despite the internationally shared antecedents of philanthropy and paternalism, CSR has been something of a minority concern until recent decades. It was historically associated with niche companies whose founders had been committed to philanthropy or paternalism based often upon distinctive religious or ethnically based convictions, as in the UK Quaker companies Cadbury's and Rowntree's, European cooperative companies, and Indian Parsee companies such as Tata. Often motivation for responsible business reflected a blend of conviction and a distinctive business model, as in the case of the UK Boot's the Chemists, whose treatment of workers and their families, and contributions to the city of Nottingham more broadly, were aligned with their business strategy of providing pharmaceuticals for poor people.

There have been modern equivalents of these companies which combine business with social mission. The Body Shop was built around various ethical and environmental issues which in turn shaped a distinctive and successful business. In the USA, Ben and Jerry's was developed in alignment with its founders' environmental and welfare concerns. Innocent Drinks developed an ethical cum sustainable ethos around the themes of 'nutrition, ingredients, packaging, and legacy'.

Interestingly, all these companies which combined social mission and business were subsequently taken over by multinational corporations (MNCs)—Oréal, Unilever, and Coca Cola, respectively. This might suggest that such responsible businesses have not only been rare but also relatively short-lived. On the other hand all three MNCs attest to the value that Body Shop, Ben and Jerry's, and Innocent have brought to their wider operations, illustrating the increasing value of that which was once marginal to the contemporary business mainstream.

In the absence of a founding ethos (as above), CSR has often been mainstreamed in response to an issue or event which has shown the company in a poor light. Sometimes companies discover the limits of rhetorically based responses to criticism as their critics reveal further cases of irresponsibility. The case of Nike is instructive in this respect, as over a period of thirty years it moved from being in denial about its responsibility for working conditions in its supply chain to being an industry leader in transparency and third party assurance of its supply chain.

Even companies with good reputations for their responsibility, can undergo reappraisals of their CSR through crisis. This is illustrated by Shell which thoroughly re-evaluated its CSR policies and corporate practices following successive crises in 1995: the disposal of the Brent Spar oil storage and tanker loading buoy; the company's alleged entailment in the execution of Ken Saro-Wira; and its indirect association with human rights abuses and environmental pollution in the Ogoniland region of Nigeria. As former CEO and Chairman, Sir Mark Moody-Stuart commented, the most important lesson 'was to be more open to outside inputs and opinions'.

For many companies, the adoption and development of CSR is neither a result of a social passion nor of controversy. It is more of a question of learning and adaptation, blending an awareness of the need for social legitimacy on the one hand, and of business

Box 3 CSR media

CSR Wire (1999 USA) is a digital media platform for the news, views and reports in CSR and sustainability

Ethical Performance (1999 UK) provides news and analysis on CSR issues

Ethical Corporation (2001 UK) provides business intelligence for sustainability

The Business Respect email newsletter (2001) gives news and commentary on CSR worldwide

Corporate Knights (2002 Canada) produces corporate rankings, research reports and financial products based on corporate sustainability performance.

Corporate Social Responsibility

opportunity on the other. One indicator of the demand by companies for CSR information and knowledge is the growth of specialist CSR media (see Box 3). A key characteristic of these media is that they include critical as well as positive perspectives on business social performance.

Subsequent chapters detail various indicators of the mainstreaming of CSR among businesses.

Leadership perspectives

Although CSR manifestly reflects the work and commitment of many within companies as well as many company–society relationships, it is axiomatic that without a leadership commitment, the energies and endeavours of others are nugatory at best and counter-productive at worst.

Business leaders have been a mouthpiece for CSR particularly with the advent of the modern corporation in the early 20th century. George Perkins, a leading executive in early 20th century American insurance, steel, and banking summed up a general view that 'the larger the corporation becomes, the greater becomes its responsibilities to the entire community'. Other business leaders tended to see business and society not as dichotomized but, rather, integral to one another. Thus David Packard, co-founder of Hewlett-Packard suggested to his employees that a company's purpose is 'to make a contribution to society, a phrase which sounds trite but is fundamental'.

Business leaders increasingly pronounce on CSR and often associate this with a personal shift in perception about business and society, and subsequently a new business strategy. Ray Anderson, founder and chairman of the world's largest carpet manufacturer, Interface, realized that in the early 1990s his company had nothing to offer in the context of environmental threats and this motivated him to turn the company around to become a leader in sustainable business: 'the notion that we can take and take and take and take, waste and waste and waste, without consequences is driving the biosphere to destruction.'

In 2006, Lee Scott, CEO of Walmart, often the bête noir of anti-corporate NGOs, announced his intention to make Walmart run on 100 per cent renewable energy and produce zero waste. He later explained that the birth of a grand-daughter had put things in perspective and that 'global warming is real, now, and it must be addressed'.

These examples reflect a new set of assumptions about business social responsibility among company leaders. A McKinsey's survey (2005) found that 84 per cent of business executives believe that companies should balance profits with contributions to public good. What that balance should constitute and how it should be achieved remain critical questions. A 2013 survey of Chief Financial Officers, usually regarded as the greatest CSR sceptics, found that the majority regard CSR as 'important in their business strategies'.

But the mark of leadership is not simply recognizing new imperatives for the company but also in embedding the values and principles deemed appropriate by the Board. This is vital for a company that wants to live up to its responsibility claims. As Sir Mark Moody-Stuart comments, this is something that cannot be done with a 'rule book', rather it is about gaining 'family like' commitment to appropriate behaviours. This, he says, can only be done by leaders who are willing to discuss and debate company practices and policies with other members of 'the family' who, in turn, are not only eyes and ears of the company, but also innovators and advocates in embedding those values and principles.

Siemens is a company which has learned first-hand about both the financial and the reputational costs of corruption. Peter Löscher,

appointed CEO in the wake of the 2008 judicial findings against
Siemens, led a major policy to embed integrity throughout the
company by means of a strategy of culture change. This included
an amnesty for managers who confessed to committing bribery
and who contributed to efforts to understand and eliminate
bribery opportunities and motivations. Other elements of the
strategy included workplace initiatives, internal media devices,
and training.

Societal perspectives

CSR has not only come of age in the mainstream of business.
Another recent dynamic is CSR's expansion from being almost
entirely a business concern to an issue with which society is
more aware and engaged. As a result the activities of business
are increasingly conducted in 'the social gaze' such that business
activities and impacts are conducted in the full limelight. In this
light, in many companies' managers are encouraged to consider
it as prudent to assume that all company actions and impacts
will be made public anyway. Thus 'the social gaze' operates
as a form of 'soft regulation' of companies, such that social
expectations can inform responsible business behaviour without
recourse to legal regulation.

Whether as a cause or an effect of these developments, public
opinion on questions of business responsibility is now tested
and expressed. The most famous such public opinion poll was
the Millennium Survey on CSR of 25,000 people in twenty-three
countries in six continents. This provided overwhelming
evidence of public expectations that business responsibility
should increase, showing that business responsibility
constitutes a more critical focus for people's estimations of
companies than corporate branding or financial performance,
and that over half the respondents attend to companies' social
behaviour. Moreover, respondents were not satisfied with a
CSR that was merely concerned with charity or community
donations: CSR should also encompass such issues as labour

practices, business ethics, responsibility to society at large, and environmental impacts.

Trend data show that social concern about the responsibility of business is also increasing. Whereas forty years ago, 60 per cent of UK respondents agreed 'the profits of large companies help make things better for everyone who uses their products and services', over the last two decades only about a quarter of respondents agree. Moreover, in their evaluations of the ethics of companies, the public appear very sensitive to particular issues, such as executive pay, bribery and corruption, or hard economic times.

One clear change which enables members of the public to maintain an effective gaze on business activity is the growth of general media coverage of business responsibility and irresponsibility. Although difficult to quantify it appears that mainstream media organizations have increased their coverage of CSR issues, as indicated by dedicated sections in newspapers, TV and radio programmes, and specialist journalists. Moreover, new media enable a much wider public engagement with CSR (Chapter 4).

The civil society sector has become much more engaged with business responsibility and irresponsibility over the last decade. Some NGOs like Christian Aid and Corporate Watch have focused on corporate claims about their responsibility as a basis for criticism. Some of the NGOs have been particularly adept at using new media as a means of engaging with business responsibility issues, as illustrated by Greenpeace's campaign against Nestlé's impact on orang-utans' habitat in Malaysia via a spoof YouTube Kit-Kat advertisement.

These developments indicate that at least in societies served by a relatively free and open media, public opinion is increasingly attuned to issues of business responsibility and irresponsibility, which means that CSR is all the more valuable for companies seeking to secure and build on a social licence to operate.

From corporate-centred to corporate-oriented

As well as becoming more mainstreamed, a leadership agenda item, and a matter for societal attention, paradoxically, CSR has also shifted from being corporate-centred to corporate-oriented. Thus whereas the CSR was originally about companies deciding for themselves what their responsibilities are and how to pursue them, it has shifted to a broader concern in which civil society and government are involved in defining and securing the responsibilities of business (Box 2).

For most of the 20th century CSR was usually 'corporate-centred' in the sense that the corporations were the key actors: it was the corporations alone whose responsibility was described in CSR; moreover, the corporations decided what their responsibilities consisted of, even if with reference to very general, usually implicit, social expectations. Finally, they tended to enact these responsibilities themselves, whether by simply making philanthropic financial contributions to worthy causes or by providing social infrastructure for their workers and their families.

In contrast, today CSR has become more 'corporate-oriented' reflecting three main developments. First, the agendas of CSR have extended beyond the activities of corporations themselves to include their supply chains—famously in textiles, timber, and fish—and their downstream effects. The most conspicuous examples of downstream responsibility include the re-use or disposal of products and packaging by customers, and the direct effects of product usage on customers, currently alcohol, sugar, and fatty foods. Secondly, corporations now respond to external assessments of what their responsibilities should include. This could be broadly through eligibility criteria for joining a CSR organization or being listed or ranked as compliant with a CSR standard. More narrowly, this could be through company-specific stakeholder input or reaction to external critique. Thirdly, CSR is more corporate-oriented than corporate- centred because other actors are involved in governing and managing CSR policies and resources. This is usually through partnerships that CSR entails with other businesses, NGOs, and governments. This could be to regulate and make transparent corporate supply chains through ethical and fair trade initiatives; to combat disease and poverty in partnership with development charities and agencies, or to regulate the use of scarce resources through stewardship councils. This development is in tandem with wider changes in civil society and government.

There has been a turn in NGO behaviour from simply being antagonistic towards corporations. Instead many now seek to induce and pressurize companies to address problems, particularly developmental and environmental, that governments have proved unwilling or unable to address. Many mainstream NGOs have seen CSR as an opportunity to draw business into their causes, be it human rights (Amnesty International), famine and poverty relief (Oxfam), or the environment (the World Wildlife Fund for Nature).

Companies have also been keen to work more closely with civil society organizations to improve their community and charity engagement. As companies have become more concerned that their community impacts are effective and socially acceptable, they have increasingly used community, charity, and NGO partners to identify key issues for companies to address, to design appropriate strategies for, and to deliver company resources efficiently and appropriately.

Governments whether of social democratic (e.g. Sweden), liberal (e.g. UK), or socialist (e.g. China) orientation have introduced policies on CSR. So too have governments as different as post-apartheid South Africa, India, Indonesia, and Singapore.

These policies range from endorsing CSR, to facilitating it, to partnering companies in it, even to mandating it. They address a wide range of environmental, social, and governance issues (Chapter 4).

The participation of civil society and government in CSR has also shifted attention from individual companies' impacts to more collective issues, such as the impacts of the sports goods industry on home working conditions, of textile retailers on health and safety in Bangladeshi garment factories, and of different forms of industrial activity on the environment. As a result of these forms of civil society and governmental engagement with business, CSR is no longer simply a matter of corporate discretion nor is it simply about the activities and effects of the respective corporations. It is no longer corporate-centred. It is now about activities and impacts in the sphere of corporations. It is corporate-oriented.

This is not to say that corporations can bow out gracefully or otherwise from CSR. They remain the key actors. Their agreement and activity is the single most important ingredient in the new multi-actor CSR mix. Their activities are also regarded as critical to the upstream and downstream issues which now populate CSR debates. They possess enormous power as purchasers and as opinion-formers, and they can achieve remarkable international reach. However, the key point is that companies' decisions and activities alone are insufficient for legitimate and effective resolution of problems identified in their spheres. They require different forms of interaction with each other and with civil society and government (Chapter 5).

We have established CSR's broad meaning and traced its movement towards centre stage in business and society. In so doing we have outlined how and why CSR is an idea whose time has come. We now turn to consider the sorts of things that companies do in the name of CSR.

Chapter 2
The company level

> *Most people…would be amazed if they lifted the stone of*
> *contemporary business activity and saw the army of*
> *consultants, experts, charlatans and do-gooders scurrying*
> *around inside and outside companies trying to help them be*
> *more socially responsible.*
>
> Steve Hilton, political strategist, and Giles Gibbons,
> business consultant (2002)

In this chapter we turn from the *idea* of CSR to its *practice*,
particularly at the level of the company. We consider the
frameworks that companies use to identify and manage their
responsibilities; the practices they engage in; and the issues of
organization, integration, and performance and impact that arise
for companies adopting CSR.

Frameworks for managing CSR

There are many frameworks, often recommended by consultants,
which are used by companies to manage their CSR. Frameworks
assist companies, firstly, in thinking about what they may be
responsible for, to whom and why, and on that basis, how to
develop CSR strategies. Secondly, frameworks assist companies in
managing their organizational systems and resources in order to
consistently and coherently implement their CSR policies. Thirdly,

frameworks assist companies in the external communication of their CSR.

We consider four influential frameworks: *the CSR pyramid*, selected for its formative influence on CSR; *the stakeholder model*, designed for business strategy in general, but adopted in the CSR context; *the triple bottom line* approach, which offers a way of integrating economic, social and environmental responsibilities; and the *shared value approach* which stresses the business case for CSR.

Carroll's CSR pyramid

One of the most famous CSR frameworks is the 'CSR pyramid' devised by Archie Carroll, a professor of management. This distinguishes four types of responsibility and frames them in a hierarchy. These are: Economic, the foundation of the pyramid (i.e. to be profitable, which is required by society); Legal (i.e. playing by the rules, which is required by society); Ethical (i.e. to do the right thing, which is expected by society); and Discretionary, the peak of the pyramid (which Carroll originally called 'Philanthropic' i.e. be a good corporate citizen, which is expected and desired by society).

Notwithstanding criticisms that this model is overly descriptive, its first strength is its simplicity. Next, by founding the pyramid on economic responsibility, it reminds us that CSR extends to the core business. This raises questions of responsibility in *how* the profits are made, rather than just what is done with them. Finally, it stresses that effective CSR is predicated upon business profitability. However worthy, the UK Woolworth's CSR policies were unsustainable once the company went into liquidation. Many of the subsequent debates about CSR have been about the relationships between how companies should manage tensions that arise between the economic, the legal, the ethical, and the discretionary responsibilities.

Carroll supplements his CSR pyramid in two ways. First, he distinguishes the types of social issues to which companies might need to respond: 'shareholder; occupational safety; product safety; discrimination; environment; and consumerism'. Thus Carroll underscores the significance of the identification and management of non-market agendas for businesses, and he anticipates stakeholder management (below). Second, Carroll distinguishes different business responses to such issues: 'proaction; accommodation; defence; and reaction'. Here he anticipates the development of strategic approaches to CSR issues.

The stakeholder approach

Another major impact on business thinking about CSR has been 'stakeholder management', mobilized and popularized by R. Edward Freeman, a professor of business ethics and consultant to companies. Stakeholders are those upon whom the firm depends for its success and who are affected by its fortunes. Companies employing this model prioritize stakeholders according to the nature of the company and its business. Thus, primary stakeholders tend to be regarded as investors, employees, suppliers and customers, and, depending on the business, government and communities. Secondary stakeholders might include the media and civil society organizations.

Stakeholder management presumes a virtuous circle by which business is best served when the interests and values of all stakeholders are accommodated in company practices. Accordingly the company is rewarded with willing investors, suppliers, and employees; loyal customers; and legitimacy among communities and governments. Together these positive alignments are assumed to be the recipe for commercial success. Thus stakeholder management aims to combine good management and ethics.

Although Freeman stresses that stakeholder management is not intrinsically about CSR, his model has been adopted by countless firms as a way of thinking about their responsibilities. Starbucks, for example, sums up its approach to global responsibility: 'Above all, Starbucks believes in engaging, collaborating and openly communicating with our stakeholders.' Many companies design their CSR reporting around 'stakeholder dialogue' as illustrated by British American Tobacco:

> The ways in which we engage with these groups include formal stakeholder dialogue sessions, long-term partnerships and customer surveys, along with day-to-day dealings such as the relationships our trade marketing representatives have with retailers or the agronomy support we provide to farmers.
>
> Engagement with stakeholders guides the continual improvement of our policies, procedures and ways of working. It provides numerous benefits for both us and our stakeholders, ranging from better relationships with our retailers to improved crop yields for our tobacco farmers.

Some problems may arise in applying the stakeholder model to CSR. First, the status of 'the natural environment', a core element in CSR thinking, is tricky. It is unclear who speaks for the environment and accordingly how its interests and values (assuming these notions are even applicable to the environment) are served by companies using a stakeholder model. It could also be contended that in reality companies have a stake in the environment rather than vice versa.

A second, and related, concern with the stakeholder model as a basis for CSR is that broad societal impacts of companies get underestimated in an actor-centred model like stakeholder management. Critics of British American Tobacco would point to the negative health impacts of their products. Critics of Starbuck's would point to its free-riding on UK taxpayers through its strategic tax minimization policies. Interestingly, this criticism has been taken on board by Starbuck's in its decision to better align its taxation payments with its UK profits.

The strengths of the stakeholder approach for CSR are that it identifies *to whom* companies are responsible and stresses that responsible business is about finding solutions which reflect the interests and values of specific actors, or 'people' as Freeman would say. Moreover, the stakeholder model challenges the 'separation thesis' entailed in the assumption of a choice facing companies and managers of 'business success versus ethics'. It thereby offers a basis for thinking in terms of the 'business case for CSR': if a company is responsible to its stakeholders it will be rewarded in business terms.

The triple bottom line

Another approach to CSR adopted by companies is the 'triple bottom line' of the three Ps: 'profit, people, and planet' developed by John Elkington of the UK consultancy, SustainAbility. The assumption is that companies should not only attend to the bottom line of the financial accounts, but they should also take account of their social and environmental impacts. This approach also assumes that there are critical interactions among these three Ps which companies need to understand to be sustainable.

There are obvious problems of commensurability in integrating business, social, and environmental performance measures and in estimating their interactions. However, this approach has been welcome for the power and simplicity of its message, and has been used in CSR reporting, management accounting, and, more broadly, by companies which are extending their CSR to connect with broader sustainability agendas. For example, Procter & Gamble's Supplier Environmental Sustainability Scorecard enables the company to measure and reward its suppliers' sustainability, focusing on their energy and water use, waste disposal, and greenhouse gas emissions. This is designed to enable Proctor & Gamble to better achieve its long term vision of:

Plants powered by 100% renewable energy; 100% renewable or recycled materials for all products and packaging; zero waste from factories or consumers going to landfills; products that delight while maximizing conservation of resources.

More widely, the triple bottom line approach has been adopted by the UN as a standard for urban and community accounting. The Global Alliance for Banking on Values which promotes ethical banking, stipulates as one of its three criteria for membership a commitment to 'social banking and the triple bottom line of people, planet and profit'.

Shared value

Michael Porter and Mark Kramer (consultants, popular contributors to the management practice literature, and, in Porter's case, a business school academic) suggest a 'shared value' approach to business. Although Porter and Kramer contrast this approach with that of CSR, it is reminiscent of, and has been adopted in, some companies' CSR thinking.

Shared value draws on the stakeholder logic but focuses more on the objective of shared value as a source of innovation and competitive advantage for companies rather than on the method of managing for stakeholders. Porter and Kramer particularly recommend companies to reconceive their products and markets, in order to produce what societies need; to redefine productivity in the value chain, so as to maximize positive and reduce negative impacts; and to encourage local cluster development, to reap the benefits of network approaches to business and societal wider problem solving.

Many CSR academics and professionals find that this approach brings little new to CSR thinking. Some would go further and criticize its excessive orientation to the interests of the company. However, it has been welcomed in some business circles precisely because it does couch CSR in terms of business success rather than responsibility alone. It is therefore attractive to companies keen to identify, maximize, or demonstrate the financial value added through making social and environmental investments.

Nestlé offers a good example of how the shared value idea can be deployed:

> we believe that, to succeed as a business in the long-term and create value for our shareholders, we must also create value for society. Our aim is to provide safe, responsibly produced food and beverages of the highest quality. But we must do this in a way which protects natural resources for future generations and ensures the people and communities along our supply chain prosper.

The Nestlé approach to shared value is presented as a pyramid, suggesting a hierarchy with 'Compliance' at the base; with 'Sustainability: protecting the future' at the second level, and 'Shared Value: nutrition, water, rural development' at the apex.

There are many more frameworks for CSR as the numerous CSR consultants (over a hundred in the UK alone) seek to differentiate themselves with a distinctive framing of CSR. We have considered four influential approaches which together address four key CSR questions: *what* companies are responsible for (Carroll's pyramid), *to whom* they are responsible (stakeholders), how economic, social and environmental considerations interact (the triple bottom line), and how CSR can make for good business (shared value). We now turn to look more closely at what companies *do*.

Doing CSR

The UK business association, Business in the Community (BITC), distinguishes CSR practices according to their respective spheres: community; workplace; marketplace; and environment. These spheres have been widely used to distinguish and organize company CSR practices, and are adopted below. There are overlaps among these spheres. For example, company actions to secure supply chain workers' human and labour rights could be described as in the workplace and in the marketplace. Moreover, CSR practices in one sphere can often be enacted in order to enhance the company's reputation in another sphere.

Responsibility in the community

Community is CSR's conceptual, historical, and practical core. It is a particularly popular CSR sphere among small and medium-sized enterprises (SMEs), reflecting both their comparatively modest reach and impact, and their frequent reliance on a local identity as part of their business reputation. However, multinational corporations' (MNCs) reputations for sociability may also critically depend on their community impacts, as Union Carbide (following the Bhopal disaster) and BP (following the Deepwater Horizon, Gulf of Mexico disaster) can attest. Thus, although CSR in the community is often disparaged as a tax-free publicity opportunity, it remains integral to many MNCs' policies. As a result, responsibility in the community has been developed into a more strategic, socially oriented, and effective sphere of CSR.

Companies often see 'community' as synonymous with society. This is because legitimacy with a company's neighbours is regarded as vital to its social licence to operate. This can influence the willingness of employees to work for them and customers to buy from them. Social licences to operate can also meld into legal licences to operate when companies seek planning permission to locate or extend premises and operations.

From the late 19th century governments in developed countries assumed greater responsibility for the community issues which corporate philanthropy and industrial paternalism had addressed, such as housing, libraries, education, and social amenities. Nonetheless, the community remains a CSR cornerstone. This was justified by *The Economist* in describing Marks and Spencer's community work during the UK 1981 urban riots as:

a sensible long-term investment in its marketplace. If urban disorders become a regular fact of life, many of its 260 stores would not survive.

It is part of the folklore of this period that Marks and Spencer's stores were undamaged when other high street shops were vandalized.

Key issues in contemporary CSR in the community include education, long-term unemployment, the environment, health, homelessness, preventing reoffending, support for employees who are also carers (e.g. for the elderly, the long-term sick), and support for social enterprises. Charitable giving, in cash or in equipment and facilities, remains a key method, but there has also been conspicuous growth in employee engagement, cause-related marketing, and long-term partnerships as modes of community responsibility.

Companies align employee engagement with CSR in the community by organizing activities and allocating work time and other resources to these. This includes employee fundraising (from sponsored activities in work time to payroll giving schemes), and 'team challenges' which address some community task (e.g. repainting a school) thereby contributing to morale and team-building. There has been a significant growth in employee volunteering (e.g. two days work time per year) through community organizations. That these schemes often have a marginal net impact on community problems and company capacities, confirms their value to companies as vehicles for employee loyalty and motivation.

In contrast, longer term secondments to community organizations combine substantial benefits for the community (e.g. in local amenities, environment, capacity-building); the individual employee (e.g. professional development) and the company (e.g. knowledge and network capacity, community reputation, employee satisfaction). Another growth area has been cause-related marketing in which companies, particularly in the retail sector, are able to bring their marketing power to support charity fundraising.

Cross-sector partnerships have become a key feature of CSR in the community. Thus instead of unilaterally diagnosing and addressing community problems, companies work in new partnerships, which involve companies in new local institutions and, often, even in supporting new business models such as social enterprises.

The size of corporate community contributions can be substantial. For example, the 300 members of the UK London Benchmarking Group reported that their contributions rose from £1.1bn in 2007 (of which 70 per cent was in cash) to £1.65bn in 2012 (of which 54 per cent was in cash). Non cash contributions can include premises, equipment, and employee time. And these figures probably underestimate the significance of business knowledge in business–community partnerships.

Many companies now approach their CSR in the community more strategically than by simply making annual philanthropic gifts. For example, many use standards to manage, measure and report their activities to address community problems. Many also align their community activities with their core business, be it by utilizing their core resource (e.g. financial institutions and micro-banking, pharmaceutical companies and combating disease), or by addressing stakeholders through their community investments. Box 4 depicts key community policies of mining giant, Anglo-American.

Responsibility in the community has developed considerably. Although philanthropy still features almost universally, it has been complemented by other activities which reflect greater

Box 4 Anglo-American's responsibilities in the community

The communities where we operate are crucial to Anglo-American's success . . . we are often vital to their growing prosperity. Mutual dependence makes it only natural that we want to make positive and enduring contributions to our hosts. Being a good neighbour is good business.

Technologies to treat excess, polluted coal mine water into drinking water, and to convert gypsum residues into energy-efficient building materials.

Support for SME development in South Africa.

Free treatment programme for employees and dependants with HIV/AIDS.

Socio-Economic Assessment Toolbox (SEAT), an impact assessment & management planning process.

engagement of companies with communities and closer alignment of this work with their core business.

Responsibility in the workplace

As some of the most notorious cases of corporate irresponsibility, such as working conditions, pay, or sexism, relate to the workplace it is little surprise that companies which value their reputation realize the importance of responsibility to their employees. Equally, as evidence mounts about the links between employee motivation and the social reputation of companies, many companies recognize that responsibility in the workplace can be about more than damage limitation, but also an investment.

The growth in workplace responsibility policies in Western countries is in one sense ironic. After all, many of the workplace responsibilities included in CSR—including working age; remuneration; labour standards; collective bargaining; health and safety; equal pay/treatment; discrimination; training; leave; and unemployment, health, and retirement insurance—reflect areas in which governments have regulated over the last century or so.

The inclusion of such issues in CSR agendas reflects several factors. First, there has been some deregulation of the workplace by many governments over the last thirty years or so (e.g. labour rights, minimum pay, apprenticeships). Secondly, some of the CSR workplace agendas also reflect the limits to regulation (e.g. equal pay/opportunity). Thirdly, new workplace issues have arisen which are not fully addressed by regulation (e.g. work–life balance, immigrant workers; harassment, whistle-blowing). Finally, globalization has put into sharp relief the workplace practices of Western MNCs abroad, where they are out of the reach of their home-based regulators. This has prompted a major new theme in CSR as companies have developed systems to address international human and labour rights for their workforces outside home country jurisdictions.

Some companies have developed diversity policies which align social and business goals by targeting sections of the workforce which might have been undervalued. One example is to focus policies on women employees in order to win their loyalty (e.g. work–life balance for those with caring responsibilities outside work, policies to encourage women to return to work after maternity leave). Other companies have recruited older, often part-time workers, on the assumption that their experience is an asset. A more recent workplace concern has been employee health and well-being which can include policies to moderate the adverse effects of physical activities, to identify and address issues of mental health, and to assist employees in financial planning.

This attention to workplace responsibility even among companies in relatively well-regulated labour markets is often explained in

> ### Box 5 Ford Motor Company's responsibilities in the workplace
>
> *The more we embrace our differences within Ford—diversity of thought, experience, perspective, race, gender, faith and more—the better we can deliver what the customers want and the more successful Ford will be.*
>
> Support employee networks that foster: diversity & inclusion; diversity & inclusion activities (e.g. 'town hall' meetings, training, summits) to foster a respectful & inclusive environment; support work/life flexibility (e.g. remote working technology, mentored flexitime, child-care facilities, nursing mothers' rooms); anti-harassment & discrimination policies; complaints procedures.
>
> Business plans in five-year increments with sustainability targets.
>
> Sustainability targets including employees' individual performance metrics.

terms of 'the war for talent'. In the context of increasing evidence that graduates, in particular, have a strong preference for working for responsible employers, CSR is often used to project the human face of company. Strategies include building CSR into staff development activities to ensure there is employee awareness/involvement in CSR and to understand how employee needs are fulfilled. Box 5 captures policies at Ford Motors for diversity and engaging the employees in sustainability.

Responsibility in the marketplace

The expectation that business should be responsible in its marketplace is in one sense uncontroversial. However, over the last two decades, there has been greater recognition of the effects of corporations' 'upstream' (i.e. through their supply chains) and 'downstream' (i.e. through impacts of their products on customers; the disposal of products) CSR activities. These had hitherto gone rather unnoticed on the assumption that suppliers were responsible for their own business operations; and that customers, particularly consumers, were responsible for how they used and disposed of corporations' products.

The social gaze has particularly focused on MNCs' *upstream* market practices in developing countries given that one of the key drivers for globalization has been the availability of cheap and poorly regulated labour. As a result, many companies have sought to address issues of labour standards, health and safety, and remuneration in supply chains in the light of their controversy in the last two decades. Equally, companies have become more aware of the advantages of creating reliable, trust-based and mutually rewarding supply chains and are thus extending CSR to these, strictly, extra-company concerns (including in local and regional supply chains).

Policies usually include reference to International Labor Organization (ILO) codes and various multi-actor standards and partnerships (Chapter 5). Most leading CSR companies employ auditors of their first-tier suppliers and in some cases (e.g. Nike) these reports are published. Whereas there is pressure on companies to 'police' their supply chains, many also take a more developmental approach by supporting and training suppliers in compliance with the agreed standards, and investing in childcare, educational and other community projects.

The impact of company sourcing policies on the environment has also become a key 'upstream issue'. Thus companies include environmental criteria in their purchasing decisions, particularly regarding sustainable sourcing of scarce natural resources, ranging from fish to timber.

Interestingly the logics of some of these expectations of CSR in international supply chains have also been applied within MNCs' home countries. In the UK, for example, CSR has been extended to policies which support domestic agricultural suppliers by attending to long-term livelihood issues as well as simple price and operational considerations. Likewise, in the wake of the 'cockle pickers tragedy' when Chinese labourers collecting shellfish were drowned, UK CSR policies have included reference to avoiding domestic suppliers who include underpaid, even slave, labour. Often these policies are also linked to marketing strategies for sustainable consumption among customers.

Box 6 introduces the Swedish fashion retailer H&M's supply chain policies for its first-tier suppliers. As is common, H&M's impact on second-tier suppliers (e.g. fabric, yarn suppliers) is much more limited but does include a Mill Development Programme.

More recent attention has been given to the *downstream* effects of business and the responsibility that companies take for product usage and disposal. Again, companies are not the only responsible

Box 6 H&M's supply chain policies

Our approach is to use our influence wherever possible to promote good practice and raise awareness, not only among our suppliers and their employees as well as others along our value chain. We believe that working together in partnership is the best way we can make a positive difference.

H&M Code of Conduct for suppliers, monitored through a Full Audit Plan (e.g. exclusion of forced & child labour; freedom of association; payment of at least minimum wage; fundamental safety provisions; chemical restrictions; wastewater treatment; full transparency; full access for inspection).

In-house auditors conducting full & follow-up audits, including of management systems.

Member of the Fair Labor Association.

actors in consumption and disposal issues. But numerous businesses have made greater efforts to exploit their powers of information provision and taste-formation to change the behaviour of others, particularly to encourage more sustainable consumption.

Companies selling products deemed dangerous or risky (e.g. containing alcohol, sugar, tobacco, unsaturated fats) have gone to greater lengths to advise consumers on safe consumption patterns, be it with information on packaging, labelling, or in media campaigns. In some cases, these companies have acted 'ahead' of regulators, perhaps intending to offset rules that might damage business prospects. In other cases, companies have acted within initiatives in which governments participate. Many companies build this into their marketing, particularly to signal the healthy attributes of their products (e.g. Danone). Some provide wider information about how their own product could fit into a healthy diet (e.g. Innocent Drinks).

CSR policies also address issues of the disposal of products and packaging. These range from information about the disposal of fast-food containers and plastic bags, to ways to dispose of or re-use IT equipment. A particularly challenging issue is to encourage consumers to return unused pharmaceutical products rather than leave them vulnerable to misuse or to contaminate water tables by disposal via WCs.

Box 7 presents IT company, Hewlett Packard's, responsibilities for re-use and disposal of redundant equipment. It includes an example of a 'closed loop' policy whereby equipment that has become redundant for the consumer is re-used in the manufacture of new items, incorporating new features.

The upstream and downstream marketplace CSR issues appear paradoxical. On the one hand they reflect the enormous power and reach of corporations, but on the other hand they point to the

Box 7 Hewlett Packard's responsibilities downstream

We are committed to helping our customers recycle responsibly, recovering 2.8 billion pounds of products since 1987.

Product return & disposal policies for remanufacturing IT hardware and recycling non-reusable products.

Trade-in policies in purchase of new HP equipment.

Return for cash policies for consumer and business equipment.

Donation policies for unneeded equipment to charities.

Equipment and data destruction services.

limits of CSR as corporate-centred. It is therefore significant that many of the examples raised in this section involve companies acting collaboratively with other businesses, with civil society and professional organizations, and with governmental agencies. They illustrate the possibilities of CSR increasingly being about co-responsibility, and that much CSR now reflects wider institutionalization of responsibility rather than simply reflecting company-based whims or habits (Chapters 4 and 5).

Responsibility in the environment

There has been extensive and growing environmental regulation, concerning use of water and forestry resources, for example, since medieval times and particularly over the last century in Western countries. concerning the effects of industrialization). Yet most conceptions of CSR and most firm-based CSR policies also prioritize the environment.

There is something of an odd fit here. First, the environment is only indirectly represented by stakeholders. Whilst nature is said to speak for itself, the meanings of its messages are far from clear. Secondly, whilst the environment is an issue in community, workplace, and marketplace contexts, it tends to get separate CSR treatment. This may be because of its intrinsic sensitivity and symbolic potency as illustrated by testimonies of the business leaders explaining radical shifts to CSR. Perhaps the environmental focus also reflects the effectiveness of environmental NGOs. Moreover, environmental impacts are easier to measure and communicate than most social and economic ones.

The policies which companies describe as their environmental responsibility address company impacts on natural resources and environmental by-products of their processes. They tend to include conservation or restitution of natural resources affected by corporate activities, or sometimes simply in the corporations' communities; the air- or water-borne emissions resulting from the corporations' activities; the consumption of natural resources in the corporations' activities; and various forms of environmentally friendly products and services.

The greatest recent growth in responsibility for the environment has probably been in the area of consumption of natural resources. Investments here have usually allowed participating companies, like Walmart, both to demonstrate a tangible impact, say on energy supplies, as well as to make long-run cost savings. Some companies have acted to assess the overall impact of their consumption of these resources and to develop corresponding policies to ensure that this consumption is sustainably managed: Unilever's and Coca-Cola's policies for water consumption provide examples. Other companies have joined stewardship councils in order to ensure that their consumption of fish, timber, and agricultural products meets standards deemed sustainable (Chapter 5).

As noted in the other spheres of responsibility, many of the leading companies have been adept at aligning their environmental policies with their marketing of products. This is reflected in the ways in which companies have marketed the environmental attributes of products ranging from cars to bottled water.

Box 8 presents UK food retailer Waitrose's responsibility for sustainable food which primarily addresses environmental issues. Overall, it can be concluded that CSR for the environment has reflected combinations of intrinsic responsibility; cost saving opportunities; innovations for new business opportunities and alignment with new forms of regulation.

Company organization of CSR

Although the shift from CSR being corporate-centred to becoming corporate-oriented has meant that much CSR organization is conducted among companies and between them and civil society and government actors, companies are still the *sine qua non* of CSR. Thus the internal organization of CSR is critical to its performance and impact. In particular, such organizational issues as board responsibility and the definition and allocation of managerial responsibility are critical.

Only a few large companies have developed a board-level portfolio for CSR alone. It is usually associated with corporate governance, human resource management, or consumer affairs portfolios. Some CEOs themselves undertake responsibility for CSR. This can mean either that it is subordinated to financial performance type issues or, conversely, that it is built into corporate strategy as a core component. In some cases those with board-level CSR responsibility have direct reporting lines from CSR managers but in others, there may only be more indirect contact via a senior executive with some broader remit.

The configurations of CSR staff vary enormously as reflected in their professional labels, which can range from Community, Citizenship, and Accountability to Sustainability. Sometimes the roles are focused and functional but as CSR positions become more senior, they also involve coordination of a range of activities, including investor relations, social reporting, communications, public policy, environmental innovation, supply chain monitoring regarding human and labour rights, and community involvement.

Many companies do not rely on internal capacity alone to devise and reflect upon their CSR policies, but hire CSR consultants to help them think through strategy in general, conduct stakeholder analysis, and develop and manage reporting systems. Some of these consultants operate exclusively in the CSR area. Usually these are relatively small organizations employing between one and a dozen consultants, though some CSR business associations also sell consultancy services. CSR consultancy is also offered as one of a suite of services by large management consultancy and accounting firms. Moreover, as noted, the growth of multi-actor partnerships for CSR has usually seen the organization of CSR shared between companies and, variously, business associations, government agencies, NGOs, and community organizations.

The growth of intra-organizational CSR staff indicates a need for appropriately prepared personnel. As CSR has increased in importance from its more discretionary heritage, companies have become more concerned to be assured that their CSR managers are appropriately qualified and experienced.

As a result, there has been a steady growth in CSR courses offered at business schools over the last decade, and in some cases these have been 'mainstreamed' (i.e. built into the general course requirements). Over 500 business schools have signed up to the United Nations Principles for Responsible Management Education. Business school accreditation systems (e.g. AACSB, AMBA, EQUIS) increasingly require evidence of commitment to engage in the themes of ethical, responsible, and sustainable business. Despite these educational developments, there remains some uncertainty among companies as to what sort of qualifications and experiences are most appropriate for CSR, particularly as it has broadened from a simple community perspective to represent company-wide and even extra-company concerns.

Evidence of professionalization is emerging. In 2004, the UK Business in the Community launched the CSR Academy to provide guidance through accredited courses, workshops, peer learning, and guidelines for self-directed learning. More recently, the Corporate Responsibility Group (400 managers from 80 member companies) launched the Institute for Corporate Responsibility to 'promote and recognise the professional standing of those working in CR or sustainability roles, facilitate networking, and support our members to develop their skills'.

Company integration of CSR

Many of the criticisms of CSR have revolved around the problem that it is too easily delegated to a 'do-gooders' section of the organization rather than being reflected in the way all employees are expected to conduct company business. In part these criticisms reflect some of the organizational realities of large corporations. However, some companies have sought to better integrate CSR through all business functions with an integrative vision and mission.

UK food and clothing retailer Marks and Spencer's integrated its sustainability activities in its 'Plan A':

> We're doing this because it's what you want us to do. It's also the right thing to do. We're calling it Plan A because we believe it's now the only way to do business. *There is no Plan B.*

It aimed to integrate five sustainability goals, and one hundred specific commitments, directly into the core strategy. The sustainability goals are: to become carbon neutral; to cease sending operational waste to landfill; to extend sustainable sourcing; to be a fair partner and set new standards in ethical trading; and to help customers and employees live a healthier lifestyle. This plan was extended to encourage customers and employees to live 'greener lifestyles' and to embed sustainability into the way the company does its business. These new goals entailed the addition of another 80 new commitments. Another UK retailer, Sainsbury's, has an integrated sustainability strategy focusing on five key 'values': being the best for food and health; sourcing with integrity; respect for our environment; making a positive difference to our community; and being a great place to work.

Jaguar Land Rover, a UK vehicle manufacturer owned by Tata Motors, built its sustainability policy around investment in engineering, combining investment in community through partnerships with schools to stimulate interest and capacity in engineering; massive reductions in energy and water consumption; and investment in the sustainability performance of its vehicles.

But the integration of CSR within an organization is more than a set of well-aligned goals with the blessing of the CEO. Companies who take their CSR seriously will often need to invest heavily in developing internal communication systems to ensure that the CSR message is understood across the company, as Marks and Spencer's has done with the Plan A and as Siemens has done in order to instil understanding of regulatory, risk, and ethical implications of corruption.

Moreover, there will need to be close review of how different business functions reflect and support the CSR policies. For example, if companies wish to understand how their CSR investments impact on their performance then they need to ensure that their triple bottom line accounting systems are really integrated into their management accounting. If a company wishes to meet certain labour standards in its supply chain, then all its buyers (whose incentives are usually around price and delivery) need to act accordingly. If a company prides itself on its health and safety record, then it needs to ensure that the standards are met in newly acquired operations and in joint ventures. And so on.

Some companies have tried to integrate CSR through reward systems of remuneration and promotion, particularly for executives. However, a recent survey found that only about 10 per cent of the largest 250 companies were able to clearly link employee remuneration to performance on social and environmental issues. This might be taken as a lack of real conviction about CSR. However, it may not always be easy to identify such a company achievement with an individual performance (though the sceptic could retort that this difficultly does not appear to inhibit other individual remuneration rewards). Moreover, if companies want to create a culture such that CSR runs through 'the DNA' of the company, they may see an individual rewards system as counter-productive.

Integration of CSR remains one of the major challenges for even the most well-intentioned company.

CSR performance and impact

Companies taking CSR seriously have an interest in their social performance. One performance question concerns whether CSR is a business investment (the business case) or an expenditure? Much academic ink has been spilled on this question, along with disputes over appropriate measures of investment, of CSR performance, and of their relationships to one another. The general conclusion of the literature is that CSR expenditure probably does contribute positively to firm performance, broadly defined. Usually the positive relationships are said to be around the relatively intangible questions of morale and reputation, but also cost savings of clean technologies and new market share through responsible business or products. More conservatively, there are also business case arguments about the business benefits of compliance. Hence, the business case is not simply an academic question but also part of the armoury of consultants and CSR managers who are never so pleased as when they have persuaded the Chief Financial Officer that the CSR department is paying its way!

A second performance question, concerns the impact of CSR on the environment, society, and governance. Most of the indicators that are easily available concern business outputs (e.g. expenditure, hours of employee volunteering, numbers of targeted populations contacted). These are valuable both from a management accounting perspective as well as to give some sense of CSR 'effort'. However, they do not answer the questions as to whether CSR is making a difference to the ostensible problem; whether there may be better ways of addressing the problem; and whether the company might be better off focusing on the business, employing more people, satisfying more customers, and providing a bigger fiscal return to the society.

Moreover, it was reported in 2014 that 40 per cent of surveyed CSR companies fail to capture the overall impacts of their community programmes. Certainly impact measurement is difficult, most obviously because there are usually multiple factors acting on, for example, the ability of a long-term unemployed person to secure a job, an improvement in the capabilities of supply chain workers, and a reduction in global warming.

Nevertheless, serious CSR companies are now seeking to move from engaging with and investing in environmental, social and governance issues, to assessing and understanding the impact of their CSR contributions. We now turn to compare and consider national and international CSR dynamics.

Chapter 3
National and international developments

*Corporate social responsibility means something but not
always the same thing to everybody.*
Dow Votaw, former Business School Dean (1972)

The concept of CSR was established in the USA over the last
century. It was a rarity in the rest of the world, where it would
have seemed something of an oddity even thirty years ago, except
by some lone scholars and niche businesses. Subsequently, there
has been a global migration of CSR, but this has been neither
uni-dimensional nor uni-directional. Despite CSR's origins, it is
not a simple export 'Made in the USA'.

CSR internationalization has not been uni-dimensional because,
although the concept has international currency, as CSR
migrates it encounters various long-standing ethical traditions
with their distinctive connotations of responsible business
behaviour. CSR encounters different systems of societal
governance, reflecting different institutions and regulations
concerning the respective roles of business, government, and civil
society actors. Furthermore, as CSR travels it encounters diverse
business–society issues, reflecting the distinctive challenges facing
different countries: ranging from poverty and disease, rapid
industrialization and urbanization, internationalization, working

conditions, and corruption; to different manifestations of environmental pollution, climate change and diversity loss.

Thus, CSR has not been simply *adopted* in different countries. Rather it has been *adapted* to different national ethical and regulatory frameworks in which assumptions and systems of responsibility are framed. So, despite becoming international, CSR does not reflect a uniform set of assumptions. Notwithstanding the importance of its integrative systems, CSR also reflects a diversity of issues and approaches. International CSR does not overlay or replace previous national business–society relations. Rather they interact with one another.

CSR's internationalization has not been uni-directional. Whilst the influence of US companies (e.g. Johnson and Johnson, Ford, and IBM in Europe) and approaches (e.g. use of standards, attention to human rights) has often been significant in CSR internationalization, there have been important non-American sources of global CSR innovation. Some of these innovations, such as a key role for business associations, multi-actor partnerships, and government involvement, have reflected European approaches to CSR. There are also other non-US hubs of CSR innovation, including partnership-based supply chain investments for community development, and micro finance in Bangladesh.

In this chapter, we compare national approaches to CSR—particularly between the USA and Europe, but also within Asia and Africa—and, in so doing, also identify factors in the international development of CSR among these and other countries.

CSR's American origins

Notwithstanding long-standing business ethics traditions worldwide, the USA is generally regarded as the home of CSR. This is because the concept of specific company-level responsibilities emerged both as a management and an academic concept in the USA, reflecting related cultural, economic, and political themes.

Cultural factors

A number of cultural factors have distinguished business–society relations in the USA even from other democratic capitalist systems. First, sociologists have observed a distinctive American culture combining individualism and community-mindedness, reinforced by myths of revolution. This informs an historic American scepticism of the state. It also informs a view that government management of public affairs should be entirely distinct from the responsibility of business to create wealth.

Secondly, there has been a long-standing American commitment to the precept of stewardship, such that individuals are attributed responsibility (often on religious grounds) to make best and most responsible use of the resources with which they have been endowed. This ethos has two faces: on the one hand, a readiness to see profit-making as sociable and as a service to society, a view reinforced by the contribution of big business to 19th century nation-building; on the other hand, stewardship brought a philanthropic corollary such that those who are blessed with wealth are expected to use it for community benefits. This found its most extreme form in Andrew Carnegie's *Gospel of Wealth*: 'to make money is only half of the task, the other half is to use it well'. Whilst stewardship initially permeated thinking about individual business owners like Carnegie, it later became transposed into expectations about the modern corporations.

Economic growth and the new corporations

In the late 19th century a new breed of corporations emerged in the USA. This reflected the relaxation of previous incorporation requirements and the consolidation of corporate rights under constitutional interpretations. It was reflected foremost in the sheer size of some new corporations, particularly railway, iron and steel, and telecommunications companies, informing their role in the continental scale of nation-building. George Perkins of US Steel commented that 'the larger the corporation becomes, the greater become its responsibilities to the entire community'.

A second phase of business expansion came in the mass production movement from the 1920s, most famously associated with Henry Ford. This not only brought new consumer products to workers' families, but also new understandings of business responsibility. Henry Gannt, better known for his eponymous charts, captured a widely held view that 'the business system had its foundation in service and as far as the community is concerned has no reason for existence except [for] the service it can render.'

However, social risks of the new corporations were also identified. Corporate governance 'founding father', J. Maurice Clarke, was particularly exercised by corporations' disproportionate social and political power notwithstanding his enthusiasm for their wealth-creating potential. Such anxieties led others to conclude that managers had responsibilities for balancing community considerations with those of the corporation and its shareholders. This reflected a broader concern that corporate managers abide by the ethos of 'trusteeship'. For some, this duty of trust was to the owners alone. Others, including John D. Rockefeller (founder of Standard Oil) and H. J. Heinz, took what might be described as a 'primary stakeholder view', that managers had obligations to owners, customers, employees, and communities. Yet others viewed managers as being trustees of the general public (e.g. Frank Abrams, a later Chairman of Standard Oil). Even the scientific management movement, associated with improving business productivity, developed a 'human relations' dimension. This extended into arguments about the societal benefits of business social responsibility for employee welfare.

Despite the engagement of academics in debates about business responsibility and the concern of some business schools with questions of ethics and responsibility, CSR did not really emerge as an academic concept until the post-war period. This was most conspicuously articulated in H. R. Bowen's 1953 book, *The Responsibilities of the Businessman* (sic), which he later described as 'skeptical and cautious, though hopeful'. The book reflects two long-standing features of US CSR: religion (it appeared in a series entitled 'Christian Ethics and Economic Life') and philanthropy (the series was funded by the Rockefeller Foundation). Bowen defined business social responsibilities as:

> the obligations of businessmen to pursue those policies, to make those decisions or to follow those lines of action which are desirable in terms of the objectives and values of our society.

He saw CSR as one of several levers to raise social welfare and a middle way between socialism and laissez-faire capitalism. Bowen justified business people taking social responsibilities seriously both in instrumental terms (to legitimize capitalism) and in terms of the duties that go with corporate power and the professionalization of management.

The attention to issues of responsibility by American business leaders, commentators, and academics does not mean that it is uncontroversial, which brings us to the politicization of CSR in the USA.

The politicization of CSR

The rise of the modern corporation prompted wider debates about its social roles. The progressive era at the turn of the 20th century saw increased scepticism about the social impacts of big business. A new breed of journalists, so-called 'muckrakers' like Upton Sinclair, Ida M. Tarbell, and Lincoln Steffens, pursued an agenda for democratic accountability and equality. In this context they drew attention to cases of corporate irresponsibility and questioned assumptions about the sociability of big business.

So, despite the comparatively positive view of business in the USA, CSR was subject to close scrutiny and scepticism, not only in the progressive era, but also during the post-Great Crash (1929) and New Deal (1933–36) eras, and later in the 1960s and 1970s, as exemplified by the 'consumerism' of Ralph Nader. More recently, US NGOs and such campaigners as Michael Moore have continued the work of the muckrakers.

European CSR

Despite the moral underpinnings of Christianity for business norms, the social roles of medieval guilds, the philanthropy and paternalism of some leading 19th century companies, CSR was a minor theme in 20th century European business. Yet by the turn of the 21st century, it had emerged as a key component, at least of UK, Scandinavian, and Northern European business as well as a theme in societal governance. Subsequently, CSR in Europe has reflected some distinctive themes as well as some commonalities with its US counterpart.

Since late medieval times, European corporations enjoyed special rights in order to achieve public purposes such as the construction of canals and bridges. Subsequently they were extended to private purposes but were nonetheless individually licensed by political authorities. These corporations were initially related to international trade, most famously, the Dutch, British, Danish, Swedish, Portuguese, and French East India Companies which entailed joint stock ownership and limited liability.

With industrialization, business philanthropy and paternalism became associated with the owners of big companies, often inspired by the Catholic, Protestant, Quaker, or Jewish faiths. These business leaders provided above minimum wages, pensions, and holidays; below minimum working hours; schools; housing and other community amenities.

In the 20th century, as European welfare state and workplace regulation emerged, business responsibility for these issues waned. As a result, Europe saw little of the public, business, and academic engagement with CSR observed in the USA. Here lies a comparative CSR puzzle. On one side of the Atlantic, in the USA, the 20th century saw increased social expectations of business, and the articulation and management of social responsibilities by companies, i.e. *explicit* CSR. Yet on the other side, in Western Europe, expectations of the responsibilities of business tended to be associated with, or *implicit* in, wider systems for allocating responsibilities led by the state, particularly in the post-war period. Why?

Implicit European CSR

The social responsibilities of business became implicit in Europe because of the emergence of wider institutions for business participation in society and for regulation of business. These institutions tended to operate at a collective, rather than individual, company level. They were collective in the sense that business was represented by associations which interacted within multi-actor systems that also included government and organized labour, and in some cases agriculture. Hence there was little CSR talk in the sense of individual companies being attributed or claiming responsibility for their social impacts.

What explains this very different trajectory from the US story? The answer lies in distinctive developments of organized labour, business and government on the European side of the Atlantic.

The rise of European organized labour and its legal recognition had two profound effects. First, through their industrial power, trade unions exerted pressure on governments to regulate labour relations, working conditions, and remuneration issues. Secondly, trade unions worked with social democrats to form political parties which campaigned for national welfare programmes, libraries, the arts, and universities. When in power, these coalitions of organized labour and social democrats enacted enabling legislation for national welfare systems. Thirdly, in the immediate wake of the Second World War, there was even a view on the Conservative and Christian Democratic side of politics, that organized labour should be a participant in policy-making processes.

There is also a business dimension to this comparative story. Modern European corporations emerged during the second half of the 19th and the first half of the 20th century. However, the formations and responsibilities of joint stock companies, and the legal notions of limited liability and corporate personality tended to differ from those in the USA. Corporate ownership and governance in most of Europe tended to be rather more mixed than in the USA, with lower levels of public shareholding, and greater levels of bank, family, and cooperative finance. In this context, the imperatives for big, powerful corporations to be explicitly socially responsible as in the USA were not so pressing.

Moreover, representatives of organized business (and labour) became integrated into various macro policy-making institutions responsible for wages, monetary policy, industry policy, and even health and welfare policies in post-war Western Europe. Thus companies became involved in government policies concerning the economy, industry, trade, education and training, and social welfare, in what was dubbed 'the century of corporatism'. In some countries, notably the UK and France, there was also the expectation that the public ownership of industry would deliver socially responsible business, hardly a widely held expectation in the USA, the New Deal period apart.

In this context CSR in Western Europe can be seen to have been 'implicit' because it was embedded in wider systems of responsibility for regulation of economic activity, working lives, communities, and the environment. There was no strong expectation of individual companies having responsibilities outside these systems. Thus, some of the key workplace and welfare issues which US CSR companies saw as their responsibility were subsumed in the European business context through regulation and consensus-based public policy-making.

But the comparative puzzle has another twist: why has there been a recent trend of European business adopting explicit CSR?

Explicit European CSR

CSR has emerged as a key element in European business–society relations, as if from nowhere, and most leading European corporations now have CSR policies. The reasons for this are contested and, anyway, are country and company specific. However, several key factors can be identified.

First, there has been a relative decline in direct government action for public purposes in Europe. Moreover, there has been a conspicuous growth of business following the privatization of infrastructure, communications, industry services, and some health and welfare services. There has also been a greater use of new multi-actor models of governance which often include business.

Secondly, there has also been an increased social gaze upon corporations, particularly in sectors regarded as providing public goods. This has resulted, in part, from governmental interest in governing through targets and audits, but also from the dramatic increase in European civil society attention to business and its social impacts (Chapter 4).

Thirdly, European business has been subject to new international understandings about management, particularly regarding the regulation, norms, and knowledge in and about business. Thus whilst the national differences in CSR remain important, they are also overlain by, and interact with, increasing international institutionalization of management standards and practices—including a plethora of new voluntary and self-regulatory initiatives which encourage more explicit CSR. These emerge from such established organizations as the UN, the OECD and the International Standards Organization (ISO), as well as new standards organizations such as the Global Reporting Initiative and various stewardship councils (Chapter 5). Of course, membership of, or compliance with, these new organizations and standards requires an explicit commitment, which is one explanation for the recent increase in European CSR.

In this context, companies are increasingly prone to seek legitimacy for their actions through following 'best practices', and in the CSR case this is illustrated in the work of the new business associations for CSR. There are new norms about legitimate business (e.g. human resources management, purchase and supply, accounting), emanating from professions and business consultancies, as well as greater levels of attention to ethical, responsible, and sustainable business in business school accreditation systems.

European and US CSR compared

Although many leading European companies have adopted the language and practices of CSR, they also retain distinctive features and bring new dynamics to CSR in comparison with CSR in the USA. As a result, a few comparisons stand out.

First, US CSR tends to stress the underlying values of CSR, whereas in Europe there is more emphasis on broad stakeholder relations and integration with strategy. CSR in the USA gives relatively greater prominence to the community sphere than in Europe, which pays more attention to workplace, marketplace, and environmental spheres. CSR in the USA tends to be more concerned with domestic rather than international issues. Where there is an international concern this tends to be around human rights, rather than climate change and transparency, for example.

American CSR is more company-based than its counterpart in Europe, where many new CSR ideas and practical initiatives reflect the work of business associations and multi-actor partnerships. Where US companies do follow collective policies these tend to be more around standards than partnerships. Finally, American CSR tends to be distanced from governmental responsibilities, and rarely includes partnerships with governmental organizations, whereas many European governments encourage CSR often by participation in it through a variety of policies (Chapter 5).

Box 9 summarizes key comparative features of the US and European CSR systems, particularly those in the UK, Scandinavia, and Northern Europe.

Box 9 USA and European CSR compared

	USA	Europe
History	A century of explicit CSR	Recent shift from implicit to explicit CSR
Ethos	Values	Stakeholder relations, strategy
Key organizations	Company, standards	Company, associations, partnerships, standards
Key issues	Community	Community, workplace, marketplace, environment
Spheres	Mainly domestic	Domestic & international
Government	Removed from CSR	Engaged in CSR

European national CSR systems

Notwithstanding these broad brush transatlantic CSR comparisons, there are important differences too in the national European CSR journeys.

The UK as a CSR Pioneer

The UK is seen as a CSR leader by virtue of its being an early mover, the number of leading UK companies involved, and the breadth of issues to which their CSR is addressed. A number of factors explain this. First, the UK and USA share some key business system features, notably their corporate governance systems and the extent of publicly-traded shareholding. There had also been some lingering attention to CSR in the UK, in particular among certain company leaders and management commentators, even when the issue was out of the mainstream. Moreover, the UK had long hosted US CSR leaders like IBM and Ford which provided local models of explicit CSR.

Secondly, the UK was the first European democratic capitalist country to dismantle key features of its post-war institutions. These include neo-Keynesian economic policy, collective bargaining, publicly owned enterprise, and tri-partite regulation of a range of economic issues from prices and incomes to apprenticeship training. This is significant because business participation in these forms of economic and social governance had underpinned UK's implicit CSR.

Thirdly, the UK CSR changes were associated with the social catastrophe of mass unemployment from the late 1970s rising to a crisis period in the early 1980s with over three million unemployed (over 10 per cent of the workforce even by official figures). In this unlikely setting, a CSR revolution was born. Many leading businesses perceived that their individual and collective legitimacy was at risk. They developed various community and workplace engagement policies: urban renewal projects; work experience and job training schemes; provision of work space and business advice to social enterprise projects; and executive secondments to local economic partnerships. Some of the policies were integrated into local and national government policies particularly in response to the problems of youth and long-term unemployment.

Fourthly, the UK CSR story includes two factors which distinguish European from US CSR: associations and government. In the early 1980s, leading companies formed Business in the Community, one of the biggest and longest-standing business associations for CSR. It was created to enable members to learn more about their responsibilities and how to develop and manage CSR strategies. In this period the UK governments, national and local, engaged business in governance through promoting CSR. They endorsed CSR in speeches and initiatives, they facilitated it through subsidies to CSR organizations and schemes, and partnered business in CSR initiatives to address mass unemployment. Subsequently, government CSR policies broadened to include the environment, ethical sourcing, international development, and responsible consumption (Chapter 4).

Fifthly, UK CSR reflects a strong civil society which has focused attention on such issues as labour standards in international supply chains, and has mobilized customer action through the fair trade movement, for example (Chapter 4). Moreover, charities and NGOs have also partnered companies in national and international CSR initiatives (Chapter 5).

Scandinavian social democratic CSR

Scandinavian companies also feature in international comparisons of the most advanced CSR practices. This would surprise those who simply regard Denmark, Finland, Norway, and Sweden as having state-led social democracies. However, the CSR reputations of these countries also reflect interactions of government welfare policies with domestic CSR across a wide range of community, workplace, market, and environmental issues. They also reflect the longer term emphasis of stakeholder management in much Scandinavian business, which has provided a vital underpinning for recent CSR departures.

Certainly, government policies for CSR are significant, and Denmark and Sweden have recently mandated social reporting for large companies. Other government policies related to international supply chains and global environmental issues, for example, reflect interactions between the internationalism of Scandinavian civil societies and the export orientation of many Scandinavian companies. As a result, one study scores Scandinavian companies particularly highly in meeting the requirements of 'the most demanding CSR initiatives'.

Northern European CSR

Many comparative studies have distinguished the Northern European, or Rhenish, countries (Austria, Belgium, France, Germany, the Netherlands, and Switzerland) from others, particularly the Anglo-American systems. This is by virtue of their post-war neo-corporatism—the role of organized labour and business in national policy-making with government. The obvious question is therefore, do these countries share a CSR model?

The evidence is rather mixed. The Netherlands and Switzerland appear to exceed the other Northern European countries in terms of their rankings on CSR indexes, membership of international CSR partnerships, and compliance with CSR standards. As in the UK and Scandinavia, the Dutch and Swiss cases combine government, civil society, and business interactions at the domestic and the international levels (and both these countries have relatively open economies).

The other Northern European countries have rather variable CSR stories. French and German companies have a mid-ranking on an index of CSR initiatives. Although France was a pioneer with its 1977 'bilan' law (requiring companies to report labour standards data to the workers' council) and the Entreprendre pour la Cité network (1986), CSR barely featured in business or government until 2000 onwards. Subsequently CSR has moved centre stage, reflecting a professional interest in responsible business, CSR research institutes, a responsible savings-fund rating agency (Vigeo), and a new government interest, including a wider requirement for social and environmental reporting under the 'New Economic Regulations' (2001). France now has the second largest United Nations Global Compact (UNGC) national company membership.

Notwithstanding its status as a green public policy pioneer and an habitual user of partnerships for public policy purposes, German business has also come to explicit CSR relatively recently. Initially CSR was seen in business as simply being inferior to the German regulated requirements for employee representation and environmental standards, for example. However, several business initiatives for CSR emerged since 2000 and these have addressed sustainable development and poverty issues. German employers' and industries' associations now promote CSR to their members.

The Mediterranean agora model of CSR

In Mediterranean countries such as Greece, Italy, Portugal, and Spain, CSR, often associated with family businesses, has grown but is less systematized and less thoroughgoing than in countries to the north. The prime focus is community and there is more modest attention to international agendas. Mediterranean CSR has been described as reflecting an 'agora' model which stresses voluntary, usually rhetorical, exchanges often underpinned by religious values. There is little in the way of established CSR systems and institutionalization. Though Spain has the largest national UNGC membership, with Portugal, Italy, and Greece, it is a relatively low scorer on a national CSR performance index.

Post-communist CSR

In Eastern Europe, former communist countries like Bulgaria, the Czech Republic, Hungary, Poland, Romania, and Slovakia have a patchy record of CSR. Polish CSR is distinctive in reflecting the ethos of the Catholic Church. In most other post-communist countries the civil society sector, including organized labour, is comparatively weak, which contrasts with the UK, Scandinavia, and Northern Europe, particularly, where civil society is critical to the defining and operationalization of much CSR. Eastern Europe is also distinctive in Europe for being the focus for international CSR initiatives designed to assist the region with transitions to mixed economies and liberal democracy.

From transatlantic to global CSR?

If CSR in Europe would have seemed counter-intuitive in 1980, it would have seemed completely impossible in most of the rest of the world, particularly where democracy, liberalism, and market economies were not embedded. Yet CSR is now worldwide as illustrated in UNGC membership (Box 10; NB: the figures in

> **Box 10 Membership of the UNGC by continent**
>
> Europe (approximately 3,500 organizational members)
>
> Asia (1,200)
>
> Latin America (1,000)
>
> North America (500; NB: the USA is the 5th highest ranked single country)
>
> Middle East and North Africa (250)
>
> Africa (250)
>
> Australasia (100)

Box 10 are not controlled by human or company population data per continent).

This internationalization of CSR is associated with several factors, which get played out differently in every country. First and foremost, whilst some of the language and practices of CSR have been 'imported', new CSR national systems are grounded in longer-standing business–society practices. Secondly, the social gaze on Western companies operating in less developed countries abroad has been strengthened. This is partly a result of changing civil society strategies and tactics, as well as their more effective international reach. It also reflects the internationalization of media, particularly of social media, permeating even China. Together they bring stories of forest degradation, sweat shops, and child labour to Western business agendas. Thirdly, the international transitions of CSR reflect greater integration of management systems of global companies and the parallel internationalization of management knowledge and practice. Fourthly, non-Western governments and companies have become more interested in CSR to better understand markets for export and investment. This knowledge is often mediated to companies through new international CSR organizations (Chapter 5). Box 11 captures the forces making for the internationalization of CSR discussed in the following sections.

Box 11 Internationalization of CSR

International language of CSR

Internationalization of the social gaze

CSR as a feature of modern management

International CSR organizations

International sources of CSR knowledge

As coverage can only be selective (and country-level guides are available), I focus first upon CSR in Asia and the Middle East where CSR interest has probably developed most rapidly in the last five years or so, and next upon sub-Saharan Africa, much of which consists of least developed countries (LDCs), where CSR is arguably most urgently needed. Of course, CSR is relatively well developed in Australasia, broadly resembling UK developments without such strong institutionalization. It is also emerging in Latin America, where it combines elements of the Mediterranean 'agora' model with some elements of USA CSR. There are memberships of some principle-based associations, notably the UNGC. Some parts of Latin America share the characteristic problems of the LDCs that I will address in the context of my review of CSR in Africa.

CSR in Asia

Whereas only 45 per cent of a sample of Asia's companies reported CSR in 2002–3, 70 per cent did so in 2005–6, and 96 per cent in 2009–10. This growth has been reflected in increased Asian membership of international associations for CSR, increased use of international CSR standards and the development of Asian organizations for CSR. The greatest, most counter-intuitive and, perhaps, most significant development has been CSR in China. Whereas CSR was barely mentioned in the context of Chinese business at the turn of the century, China is now ranked 6th for national company members of the UNGC and has seen a rapid growth in CSR reporting over the last decade.

There are also great variations in CSR in Asia. Japan has had a relatively long-standing implicit commitment to CSR, through corporations' 'lifetime employment' policies, integration of CSR with national government policy, and close and long-standing supply chains among domestic SMEs. However, this image of solidarity has been unsettled in the wake of the Asian economic crisis, prominent corporate scandals, and the greater internationalization of Japanese business. These trends encouraged greater attention to explicit CSR. Singapore, a relative latecomer, has emerged as an Asian CSR leader, following a government initiative around the turn of the century. Some countries seen as relative CSR laggards nevertheless have niches of excellence:Bangladesh, for example, is the home of the Grameen Bank's model of micro-finance for the poor; Pakistan is recognized as a place for responsible sports-wear and equipment sourcing, first enshrined in the Atlanta Agreement between the ILO, UNICEF, and the Sialkot Chambers of Commerce in 1997.

There are some key common themes in CSR in Asia, most obviously the greater attention to community matters, as opposed to production, environment, and employee issues, than is found in Europe and even North America. This reflects the cultural significance of philanthropy in many Asian business systems especially in the context of community manifestations of poverty, illiteracy, and disease. Issue focus apart, other key distinctive themes include the role of cultural values, Asian CSR initiatives, government and CSR, and Western influences.

CSR and Asian cultural values

Much of the CSR variety in Asia reflects the diversity in cultural values and related expectations of business. Japanese business has long been associated with community strength—the Japanese word for business 'keie' combining 'kei', 'governing the world in harmony while bringing about the well-being of people', and 'ei', denoting 'ceaseless effort'. Chinese CSR partly results from the retrieval of elements of Confucianism and Taoism, the former regarding social and the latter environmental responsibilities. CSR in the Philippines reflects a Christian language of responsibility.

In several Asian countries, for instance Malaysia, Indonesia, and Pakistan, as well as in the Middle East and North Africa, CSR reflects underlying Islamic cultural values and practices. The Islamic affinity between commerce and society entailed in the concept of 'taweed' (unity) presumes that there is no contradiction between profits and moral action. Property is understood as a trust ('amanah') and its uses are subject to moral limits grounded in the concept of 'khalifah' which, in business, is understood as social responsibility and stewardship. 'Riba' (non-exploitative commercial relationships) informs Islamic banking in which investors are usually rewarded with profit-sharing rather than interest. 'Zakat' assumes that adults pay a social tax to worthy recipients. Although these were traditionally distributed for the hadj, or pilgrimage, they are now more broadly dispersed according to social need, often through state agencies or industry associations.

However, Asian cultures are rarely entirely national in their coverage and thus most countries contain diverse religious and other cultural frames for business responsibility. CSR in Malaysia, for example, reflects the community orientations of Islamic, Chinese, and Indian businesses, and in the case of the latter two cultures there is sometimes an overlay of Christian ethical concepts.

This theme of national diversity of cultures influencing CSR is most pronounced in India where a myriad customary systems underpin the variety of business and CSR models. The most famous of all has been the impact of the minority ethnic group, the Parsees. Their notion of responsibility prizes obligations not only to their own community, but also to the society to which they migrated. This materialized in the Tata group, now one of the world's largest MNCs, which pioneered responsibility in the workplace and community from its inception in the late 19th century, and in social auditing in the 1980s. Jamshetji Tata stated in 1895 that Tata Iron and Steel was founded on the principles of 'considering the interests of the shareholders our own, and the health and welfare of the employees'.

Government and CSR in Asia

As in Europe, so in Asia, governments have been prominent in
CSR development. For several decades, the Japanese government
has encouraged CSR through endorsing and providing templates
for codes of conduct, and social and environmental reporting. The
Singapore government added CSR to the portfolio of the Minister
for Labour early in the 21st century.

The most thoroughgoing case of government-led CSR in Asia has,
however, been in China. Domestically, CSR was employed in the
'harmonious society' project as a means of encouraging business
contributions to the national economic, social, and environmental
agendas. This draws on the communitarian ethos expounded by
the Chinese Communist Party. Additionally, the government
encouraged exporting sectors to use CSR as a means of better
understanding and anticipating social expectations in Western
markets, as illustrated in the Environmental, Social, and
Governance (ESG) reporting requirements in the Shanghai Stock
Exchange. Subsequently, many provincial and city governments
also deployed CSR frameworks to assist companies make social
and environmental improvements in their respective jurisdictions.

The most interesting recent developments are efforts by the
Indian government to use mandatory regulation for CSR. It
introduced a CSR tax in the 2012 Companies Act requiring
specified companies to devote the equivalent of 2 per cent of their
taxation obligations to CSR. Whilst this appears to stretch the
CSR definition, the Act is likely to enable very wide discretion as
to what counts as a contribution to CSR, and thus remain
consistent with CSR's discretionary core.

Western influences on CSR in Asia

Notwithstanding the significance of the Asian-inspired CSR
developments, Western influences are also significant. This was
originally in countries where colonial companies brought European

community-oriented responsibility policies, notwithstanding other more oppressive features of their operations. More recently, the theme of globalization has seen some Western MNCs applying their product and supply-chain labour standards to their Asian suppliers.

A more counter-intuitive trend is the growing Asian appetite for learning about and joining international CSR organizations (Chapter 5). Moreover, this has spawned the emergence of a series of national CSR networks throughout Asia. The World Business Council for Sustainable Development also reflects a growing Asian membership. The FTSE4Good Index has a growing list of Asian, particularly Japanese, companies. The ISO 26000 and the Global Reporting Initiative are increasingly adopted in Asian companies.

Some Western companies operating in Asian companies also contribute to CSR development. Hindustan Unilever Limited has developed numerous projects to address poverty and women's low cultural status through innovative business models such as micro-products and 'bottom of the pyramid' investment. Also some Western companies have been prominent in disaster relief (following the China earthquake of 2008 in the Sichuan province, for example), and have been exemplars for domestic companies' development of CSR disaster policies. Moreover, there have been collective business impacts on CSR in Asia through Western Chambers of Commerce, like the American Chambers in China and Indonesia, which act as catalysts and information providers for CSR in various Asian countries. Finally, Western development and cultural agencies have assisted CSR policy development in Asia, such as the German Gesellschaft für Internationale Zusammenarbeit (GIZ) notably in China, and the British Council especially in India.

Asian CSR initiatives

There have been numerous Asian CSR initiatives illustrating the interplay between international trends and latent cultural values.

From the early 1990s, Japanese business associations began producing charters for responsible business. More recently, there have been CSR initiatives whose forms echo Western standards but whose design and justification also reflect Islamic culture including: the Malaysian Securities Commission's CSR Framework for Malaysian Listed Companies; the Saudi Responsible Competitiveness Index; and the Hawkamah Environmental, Social, and Governance Index in the Middle East and North Africa. More familiar types of initiative include the formation of associations for CSR, like that promoted by the Association of South East Asian Nations (ASEAN).

In the context of the still deep-seated problems of poverty, disease, and illiteracy in Asia, it is also significant that Asian companies have been prominent in distinctive CSR community initiatives. There have been long-standing community development partnerships between companies, NGOs, and governmental organiations in India. Secondly, the theme of community empowerment has been a prominent one. For example, Titan Industries (part of the Tata Group) addressed female infanticide and general low esteem of women in Tamil Nadu by enabling women to develop businesses in the Titan supply chain (e.g. Myrada). Thirdly, companies have been ready to devote their core resource to address a community problem. The Indian IT company, Wipro, has deployed its technology to assist in developing education in rural areas in order to empower individuals and communities, and has done so by engaging their own employees both in work time and in volunteering programmes.

CSR in Africa

South Africa apart, Sub-Saharan Africa is something of a CSR outlier given the scale of its social, environmental, economic, and political problems. Yet it is an important CSR focus by virtue of its comparative development. Stages of development can be a fraught concept in terms of political debate, particularly regarding assumptions about the causes and consequences, and methods of measurement. The UN defines least developed countries (LDCs) in terms of levels of poverty, human resource weakness (e.g. nutrition, health, education, and adult literacy), and economic vulnerability (e.g. reliance on economically unstable products). Most of the LDCs are in Sub-Saharan Africa, with others in Latin America and Asia.

In most of Africa between the Sahara and South Africa, the greatest CSR impetus comes with international trade and inward investment. The CSR interest in LDCs is often a corollary of cases of corporate irresponsibility which go with their low wage and taxation economies, and weak environmental regulation. Nigeria, for example, has received most attention in the CSR literature due to the impact of oil extraction on the Niger Delta and the Ogoni people, which also embroiled Shell in wider issues of corporate and societal governance agendas.

However, MNCs have also been associated with innovative CSR policies. These are often motivated by the weakness of African regulatory environments and the absence of reliable welfare systems, as well as more familiar development challenges such as poverty, illiteracy, and cycles of famine and disease. GlaxoSmithKline has led a multi-actor partnership, PHASE (Personal Hygiene and Sanitation Education) to address diarrhoea-related disease. It recently launched another programme in partnership with Save the Children to address causes of infant mortality in Africa. Novo Nordisk has pioneered attempts to address the problem of diabetes in Africa and elsewhere through the World Partner Project, which provides a model for organizing and assessing efforts to address diabetes. Novo Nordisk also contributes its own resources to training healthcare professionals, and to training and treating patients.

Numerous MNCs operating in Africa, from mining to communications companies, have addressed the problem of HIV/ AIDs. This has resulted from the recognition that AIDs has a huge impact on the health and longevity of their own workforces, and that their own operations have often exacerbated the spread of the disease. Responses, usually in coalitions with public health authorities and NGOs, include provision of drugs, contraceptives, clinics, and awareness-raising.

The MNCs' stress on community also reflects weak regulatory environments and low levels of regulatory enforcement in wider business arenas. There is little CSR guidance, partly reflecting a weak civil society in general and low levels of awareness and mobilization on key issues and agendas. In addition, there are relatively few options for company–civil society partnerships to design and implement CSR. As a result Anglo American developed its own Socio-Economic Assessment Tool (SEAT) for identifying and managing the company's socio-economic impact on local stakeholders, particularly affected communities (Box 4).

In addition to the role of MNCs in bringing CSR to LDCs in Africa, there has also been a growing African company interest in CSR. Some African companies have introduced CSR systems: for social reporting; integration into fair trade systems; the Extractive Industries Transparency Initiative; the Equator Principles; and the use of the International Standards (Chapter 5). The interest is mainly at the level of engagement rather than innovation, integration, and transformation. This reflects the context of low levels of management investment and buy-in, resulting in low levels of CSR knowledge and initiative. Examples of African-based CSR systems are the Ghana Business Code (2006) which draws on UN GC principles (Chapter 5) and the Business Action Against Corruption partnership.

South Africa is something of a case apart. This is related to the long-standing integration of its economy and companies with Western counterparts. However, major CSR-related innovations emerged with democratization. The first of these was the 1994 King Report on corporate governance, which made an explicit link between the principle of accountability and companies taking responsibility for social, ethical and environmental, as well as financial, practice. The Black Equal Employment Act (2003) has inspired the development of CSR-type codes of practice and performance measures (reflecting another distinguishing feature of South Africa, a relatively strong labour movement). The introduction of the Johannesburg Stock Exchange Socially Responsible Investment Index (2004) has also served to institutionalize socially responsible investment (Chapter 4).

Internationalization of CSR

So CSR has rapidly migrated from a US concern to a multinational one, and even an international one. Two qualifications need to be made to the hasty conclusion that an American template of global CSR is emerging, even though the USA was the cradle of CSR. First, the flow of ideas and innovation is by no means unidirectional. Secondly, the CSR presence in many national business systems does not make for a single, or global, system, even though CSR has clearly become more internationalized.

Looking first at the flow of CSR influence, it should be also noted that the migration of CSR ideas is not simply from the USA. European CSR has often led the way in the use of multi-actor partnerships to develop and operate CSR systems. Europe has seen much greater readiness on the part of governments to integrate CSR into wider public policy frameworks, and on that of companies to cooperate in these processes. Moreover, CSR diffusion is not simply from the West/North to the East/South. Many of the most interesting innovations—notably micro-financing, microproducts, ICT applications for development, supplier driven ethical trade, capacity building through business—have roots in Asia and Africa. These often reflect concern with fundamental aspects of empowerment or systemic reform which Western companies might be reluctant to take on 'away from home'.

Despite internationalization of CSR there is very little to suggest a global system. Rather, CSR is a multinational patchwork in which national CSR systems reflect the long-standing ethical systems associated with their distinctive cultural inheritances. Contemporary CSR agendas also reflect the material concerns of national political systems. These are usually founded upon distinctive environmental circumstances and the long-term human impacts on everything from the balance of sectors of the economy, economic development, social structures, and legal and political systems, to levels of poverty and distributions of wealth. Moreover, the aptitudes and resources of national governments and national civil societies are crucial for shaping national systems of CSR.

Another source of unevenness in the internationalization of CSR is that individual companies have very different CSR policies and programmes across countries. On the one hand this can be said to reflect the different sorts of problems facing societies in different places. However, the unevenness in international CSR also reflects the ways in which MNCs become internationally diversified as they seek to exploit specific international opportunities in different regions. Thus, on the one hand a company can contribute to the alleviation of poverty in an area of its operations, both by philanthropic contributions and by injecting cash into subsistence economies. Yet the same company can also be associated with oppressive labour conditions in its supply chains, precisely because it sought to lower its labour costs.

The phenomenon of being responsible at home but irresponsible abroad has been frequently observed. Siemens, for example, has had a strong reputation for responsibility in Germany but this coexisted with a toleration of corrupt practices abroad. In other cases, Western chemicals companies such as Bayer known for their legal business practices at home, were identified as selling pesticides in India which were outlawed in the USA and the EU, and which had seriously detrimental human and environmental health implications.

Yet this seemingly multinational character of CSR holds in it the seeds of a more genuinely international phenomenon. This is because increasingly Western companies have to give an account to their home country societies and, in some cases, even to their governments, of the impacts of their business on social and environmental conditions in host countries (Chapter 5).

As with CSR more generally, flourishes of CSR activity often follow particular cases of business irresponsibility abroad. This is illustrated by company responses to revelations of Bangladeshi child labour in Western textile supply chains in the late 1990s and, more recently, to the Bangladeshi Rana Plaza disaster. In both cases, new firm level policy commitments were made to ensure that this 'never happened again'. But even here responses vary. Many US firms, like Walmart, responded to the Rana Plaza disaster unilaterally whilst many UK, Danish, and Norwegian companies did so collectively through their Ethical Trade Initiatives (Chapter 5). Such collective systems offer the prospects of greater international CSR in that they more readily connect home country (usually Western) customers and their watchdogs, with supply conditions in host countries.

In both cases, however, by seeking to manage their cross-border responsibilities, these US and European companies draw upon and develop international CSR management practices in tandem with new international CSR organizations and systems—to which we now turn.

Chapter 4
The socialization of markets

*Unless there is a clear business case for CSR, firms will have
fewer incentives to act responsibly.*

David Vogel, Professor of Business Ethics (2005)

This chapter and Chapter 5 are both concerned with how and
why CSR has become more institutionalized. This chapter is
concerned with the ways in which CSR features in some markets,
thereby shaping a 'business case' for CSR. This is because markets
have become increasingly socialized as non-economic—i.e. social,
environmental, governance—criteria feature more often in
market transactions. As companies both respond to and reinforce
this trend, they consolidate CSR as part of 'business as usual', and
new shared and legitimized norms of appropriate business
behaviour emerge.

The socialization of markets results, particularly in socially
responsive political systems like democracies, from the interaction
of market, social, and governmental factors. The market factors
reflect changing consumer, investor, and employee values, and the
impacts of company CSR policies on markets. Social and
governmental factors reflect ways in which civil society and the
media, and governments, reshape markets so as to reinforce the
importance of social criteria. Box 12 summarizes these linkages.

Market factors

Consumer pressure for responsible business

Although corporations clearly have considerable power to shape tastes through innovation and marketing, consumers can also shape corporate behaviour. Although these preferences are usually around price and quality, consumers can also include their own preferences regarding issues such as local sourcing, organic food, animal rights, or internationalism in their purchasing decisions.

Perhaps the most well-known form of ethical consumerism involves boycotting targeted, usually branded, companies whose practices consumers collectively find objectionable: apartheid and Barclays; infant milk formula in developing countries and Nestlé; environmentalism and Shell, and animal rights and McDonald's are good examples. These boycotts are usually led by NGOs and also involve other forms of direct action like demonstrations or stunts. In these cases company responses usually range from damage limitation to engagement with critics and even concessions. Famously, though, in the 1990s McDonald's resorted to what proved to be lengthy and costly litigation against two animal rights London protestors with significant and continuing reputational damage.

Consumers have also brought their social values to shopping through loyalty to 'values led' companies. For example, the UK Cooperative Society group attracted customers who shared an attachment to social democratic values, particularly equality and internationalism, as well as commitment to the cooperative business model. More recently the Body Shop and Ben and Jerry's built customer bases around their commitments to, respectively, animal rights and international development, and the use of natural ingredients, along with other product qualities.

New mechanisms have emerged which enable customers to be loyal to particular products, and thereby to supply chains and companies, whose attributes and practices are consistent with consumer values. Fair trade entails certification, labelling, and branding of products according to specific attributes, particularly supply chain wages and working conditions, but also other social and environmental criteria.

Underpinning the prominence of fair trade is a social movement, politically or religiously inspired, of internationalism in Western countries. Yet this has progressed beyond niche markets to the high street because of the positive response of companies seeking to integrate fair trade into their CSR. Fair trade offers companies legitimacy, certification, marketing and branding opportunities, as well as the expertise in fair trade organizations addressing difficult international supply issues. Products which reflect the impact of fair trade include tea, coffee, chocolate, sugar, and bananas. More recently the product range has expanded to include flowers and wine, for example. Fair trade accounts for modest proportions of all these markets, but its share is growing. It is generally associated with the high end of the market where consumers tend to be more aware and are able to afford the cost margins often built into fair trade prices.

Through fair trade, CSR is becoming more institutionalized. For example, the Fair Trade Foundation (FTF 1992) provides an umbrella for UK international development organizations like CAFOD, Christian Aid, Oxfam, Traidcraft, the World Development Movement, and the National Federation of Women's Institutes. The FTF logos are now employed by about 350 UK retail companies, on packaging and on the products themselves and in publicity and marketing materials. They are increasingly familiar to consumers and used as a signal for purchasing. It estimated that in 2012 FTF products were worth £1.5bn: an annual increase of 18 per cent. Despite hard economic times in the aftermath of the 2007 financial crisis, fair trade continues to grow and its systems continue to become more robust.

The Fairtrade Labelling Organizations (FLO) bring together similar organizations from Europe, Japan, North America, Mexico, and Australia/New Zealand, and networks of producer organizations from Asia, Africa, Latin America, and the Caribbean.

More briefly, some major retail companies such as Waitrose, recognizing the interest of consumers in CSR, invite customers to share in decisions as to which community causes the company should support. Likewise a number of companies facilitate customers' charitable giving; Sainsbury's, for example, facilitates customer giving to such UK national charitable causes as 'Red Nose Day' and 'Comic Relief'.

Finally, many companies, particularly retailers like Sainsbury's and the Co-op, engage with customers about their responsibilities through new media, particularly through interactive features in their websites. In so doing they not only aim to better understand customer expectations but also to enhance their legitimacy as responsible companies.

Socially responsible investment

Another niche for actors wanting to bring their values to their market behaviour can be found in the socially responsible investment (SRI) movement. This has been a relatively long-lived minority phenomenon (the US Pioneer Fund dates from 1928). From the 1960s it grew into the mainly US ethical investment movement. In the last two decades it has grown in itself and influenced more mainstream thinking about CSR from an investor perspective.

Like responsible consumption, responsible investment has been transformed from being a system based on 'exclusion' to one that also enables rewarding good practice. Hence the ethical investment movement was originally associated with the avoidance of 'sin companies' such as those associated with alcohol, tobacco, arms, pornography, or racism.

Now SRI combines 'exclusion' (accounting for about 50 per cent of assets under management) with a greater emphasis on more 'inclusionary' practices. The new indexes and standards identify companies which meet (e.g. through FTSE4Good) or which excel at (e.g. Dow Jones Sustainability Index) specified environmental, social, and governance criteria. In contrast to the earlier exclusionary schemes, the SRI asset managers aim to generate long-term stability and above-market returns to investors.

SRI has grown such that it accounts for about 15 per cent of US, and about 10 per cent of European, managed asset markets. It is harder to generalize about the financial performance of SRI as it clearly varies among portfolios and from year to year. The European SRI market outperformed the overall market between 2009 and 2012.

SRI is becoming more institutionalized as new organizations have emerged. There are dedicated SRI indexes (e.g. the KLD 400 Social Index (1990), now the MSCI KLD 400 Social Index). The FTSE4Good Index Series, founded in 2001, has had between 700 and 900 international companies listed, in which time it has also de-listed about 300 companies. The Index has criteria for: climate change, environmental management; human and labour rights; supply chain labour standards; corporate governance; and countering bribery.

There is a small SRI screening industry of data providers which created about 80 new rankings and indices between 2000 and 2010. There are national SRI associations throughout Europe many of which are members of EuroSIF along with general asset managers, SRI analysts, banks like Triodos that have a social mission, and civil society organizations like Oxfam.

A more specialized SRI innovation is the Carbon Disclosure Project database which makes transparent the greenhouse gas emissions, water usage, and strategies for managing climate change, water and deforestation risks of 3,000 leading companies. This information is used by over 700 institutional investors, responsible for US\$87tn assets.

As with fair trade, so with SRI: its market power is reinforced by the eagerness of many companies to signal their CSR by means of SRI indicators. Thus, the information provided by SRI organizations is used by companies as a badge of their responsibility and by civil society organizations in their estimations of company credentials.

The SRI movement has also had a financial mainstreaming effect providing relevant data and frameworks to general investors interested in social and environmental risk. The insurance industry, for example, has become more concerned with climate change and other abnormal environmental events. Other investor organizations have signed the Equator Principles to understand and address social and environmental risk in international development projects. There are about eighty signatories from thirty-five countries, together accounting for about 70 per cent of project finance in developing countries.

Whilst SRI remains a niche activity, it is growing, becoming increasingly institutionalized, and has attracted the main financial industry players as well as the more dedicated actors wanting to use investment to socialize business. It has encouraged companies to signal their CSR both for the purposes of attracting additional capital and for broader legitimization of their CSR.

Employee values

The impact of employee values on CSR is more difficult to measure than that of consumer or investor values. However, a 2012 survey of students and workers in the Net Impact network found that having a social impact on the world is an important life goal for most people. More specifically, 45 per cent of those surveyed would take a 15 per cent pay cut to work for an organization that makes a social or environmental impact, and 35 per cent to work for a company committed to CSR. Certainly, companies repeatedly indicate that they regard employee expectations of their responsibility as a crucial factor in encouraging and even directing their activities.

The connection between employees and CSR is relevant in the broader context of the 'war for talent' in an era when lifetime loyalty cannot be taken for granted. Employees are likely to switch employers whether for remuneration, work content, life-style or, as companies appear to believe, the values that companies operate by. Thus companies signal how they meet employee expectations by entering the 'best place to work' competitions, both to reassure their current employees and attract new ones.

Companies indicate that CSR is associated with employee motivation and retention. As a result they seek to involve employees in their CSR, as evidenced by general employee attitude surveys. CSR policies in the community are particularly targeted at employees, and often enable employees to be directly involved in their own communities through volunteering or mentoring schemes sponsored by their employers. Many companies operate employee polls on preferred charities for company partnerships or philanthropy. Research suggests that this has become one of the fastest growing modes of CSR, particularly in the USA and the UK.

Whilst employee impacts on the socialization of markets are internally institutionalized, these are nonetheless taken very seriously by companies as evidenced in the workplace sphere of responsibility. Moreover, CSR business associations and consultancies provide frameworks and management systems for employee involvement in CSR, indicative of the value that companies are placing on meeting employee expectations.

Companies and the socialization of markets

Companies adopting CSR strategies need to assure stakeholders that their CSR credentials run through their value chain. As a result they often impose the social standards which they claim for themselves upon their suppliers. Thus many companies have imported or developed codes for their suppliers around, for example, their environmental impacts. Often they provide training for their suppliers and accreditation for those who meet the criteria.

Sometimes these systems are regarded as a burden by their suppliers, but they can also be recognized as part of quality improvement and some suppliers use their accreditations to win wider business. Moreover, aware of the expectations of Western companies regarding labour and environmental standards, some developing country suppliers have taken initiatives to develop their own standards for these markets thereby creating market advantages for themselves.

Finally, some companies take public stands concerning responsibility in their 'business to business' relationships. Following the revelations of the *News of the World* journalists' phone hacking, a number of companies publicly withdrew their advertising contracts from the paper, thereby hastening its demise. UK banks have publicly warned ICT MNCs that unless the internet services guarantee that children are protected from violent and pornographic content, the systems for receiving payment from ICT users will be withdrawn. Most recently five of the six main sponsors (Sony, Adidas, Coca-Cola, Visa, and Hyundai/Kia) of the Fédération Internationale de Football Association (Fifa) made public statements indicating their concern about allegations that the award of the 2022 World Cup to Qatar has been compromised, and that the allegations should be investigated. These examples suggest that companies are motivated to become more active in these more socialized markets, rather than simply reacting to societal pressure.

Social factors

The increasing socialization of markets that we have traced has not taken place in isolation. Rather it reflects wider developments in civil society, new attention of the media to business, new media modes, education, and general societal attitudes.

Civil society

Civil society organizations, particularly campaigning and advocacy NGOs, give increasing attention to the social and environmental impacts of individual companies. This contrasts with an earlier emphasis on targeting government or capitalism in general. This trend in part reflects the greater social and environmental impact of business as well as a broader reorientation of civil society strategy.

Many campaigning organizations play a key role in publicizing allegations of corporate irresponsibility through new media strategies, thereby alerting consumers, investors, employees, regulators, and the general public (who consistently indicate that they trust NGOs more than other business and governmental actors). As a result CSR is much more attuned to civil society values and approaches to problem-solving than reflecting corporate preferences alone. The interest of corporations in social and environmental risk often reflects a desire to avoid the risk of criticism from such opinion formers.

But many NGOs have also shifted from being habitual critics of business to being periodic partners, including: Oxfam and Unilever; Save the Children and Glaxo Smith Kline; Amnesty International and Business in the Community. Companies welcome opportunities for partnerships which bring legitimacy, specialist knowledge, and implementation capacity which are the unique resources of such organizations.

Some NGOs fear the dependencies that these partnerships bring given their own modest organizational capacities, or that partnerships too easily 'marketize the social'. Others report that the new interest of companies in long-term approaches to social and environmental problems brings a welcome seriousness as well as valued financial and organizational resources.

Overall, many initiatives which companies use to signal their CSR are co-designed and co-operated by civil society organizations.

The media

The role of the media in CSR reflects several key factors. First, mainstream media has given greater attention to CSR and wider sustainability issues. Thus, many newspapers have employed CSR journalists and dedicated space to CSR issues. Likewise radio and TV give air-time to these issues.

The new media made possible by new information and communications technology have affected the quantity of, and participation in, debates about business. This enables business to provide on-line social reports, and even to facilitate forums for debates about business responsibility (e.g. Shell). Critics of business like Corporate Watch are also able to bring news of business irresponsibility to their readers) as well as to dramatize their critiques of business practices as in Greenpeace's YouTube attack Nestlé's palm oil sourcing policies. Lego withdrew its promotional campaign with *The Sun* newspaper following an on-line petition of parents who object to *The Sun's* 'Page 3' topless women feature.

Governmental factors

Governments have long made rules to require business behaviour to meet societal expectations (e.g. weights and measures, labour rights, corruption). Recently, particularly in Europe, but also in many Asian countries and South Africa, governments have encouraged CSR as a more indirect form of socializing business. These initiatives do not strictly proscribe particular behaviours, but prescribe in detail what would constitute conformance with policies, or threaten punishment for failure to comply. In this light the new governmental roles can be described as 'soft law' or the 'new accountability'.

Policies for CSR vary in issue focus and regulatory strength. At the narrowest there are policies to encourage community giving, but there are also policies (notably in the UK and Scandinavia) which straddle social, environmental, economic, and international policy areas. In these cases, the governments appear to have identified CSR as a complement to more traditional public policies as it brings company resources to address public problems and obviates short-run compliance costs.

Endorsing CSR

The lightest touch approach by government to CSR is simply to endorse it. This will attract those companies which are either grateful for authoritative guidance on responsible behaviour or keen to maintain a good reputation with government, whether to avoid regulation or to be a preferred supplier to public authorities.

Michael Heseltine, UK Secretary of State for the Environment, 1979–83, successfully enjoined business leaders to contribute to the challenge of bringing down mass unemployment and reversing urban decay during the 1980s recession. German ministries host websites related to CSR and sustainable development. Many governments encourage CSR by adding their imprimatur to CSR initiatives such as training schemes and awards, as in the case of the Austrian awards for equal opportunity and family friendly schemes, or the Bulgarian awards for socially responsible enterprise.

Facilitating CSR

Governments also facilitate CSR initiatives through subsidies to CSR organizations or schemes, and through tax incentives for CSR expenditures (e.g. historically under Charities Acts). Recent examples include tax subsidies in Sweden for employee giving schemes; the adoption of clean technologies in the Netherlands; and the employment of disadvantaged workers in Hungary. Governments also use public procurement policies to require their suppliers to reflect CSR criteria, hence shaping markets through public expenditure. Governments can either design the criteria themselves, as in Northern Ireland where requirements for religious diversity in workforces were imposed upon companies supplying the government, or they can choose to adopt existing standards as the UK did in the case of the Forest Stewardship Council.

Partnerships for CSR

Many governments encourage CSR by creating partnerships. Early examples were local economic initiatives through which companies are enjoined to collaborate in addressing local economic downturns. Most of these partnerships reflect business, government, and civil society membership and have been particularly prominent in countries like the Netherlands and Scandinavia, where governments have long used partnership models for public policy more generally. Numerous governments, such as Germany and Italy, have introduced CSR multi-stakeholder forums to encourage wider partnership approaches to CSR. (In Chapter 5, I show how government-inspired partnerships feature among leading international CSR organizations).

Mandating CSR

Finally, governments have used their powers of mandate to encourage CSR. Unlike more general cases of stipulative and coercive business regulation, these examples usually allow a great deal of discretion in the interpretation of, and compliance with, the respective mandates. Probably the most common such use of mandate has been in regulations in stock exchanges requiring environmental, social, and governance reporting of listed companies. This includes Johannesburg, New York (notably through the Sarbanes–Oxley and Dodd–Frank Acts in response to corporate and accounting scandals, and the financial crisis, respectively) Paris, Shanghai, and Australia where a requirement to report gender diversity is included. This trend has been followed by more regulation for public CSR reporting of companies as in Denmark and Sweden, and pension funds as in France and the UK. They have also been used in South Africa to improve equal access to employment, in the EU in the creation of carbon markets, and in India to promote philanthropy.

Virtue in markets?

The findings of this chapter will encourage those who see markets as the appropriate means of regulating business. They will prize the opportunities for markets to be nudged or even revolutionized, without wholesale regulation, noting that the governmental roles in CSR are more about fine tuning than about heroic efforts at socializing the economy such as public ownership, planning, and controls.

The trends do indeed constitute a remarkable feature of the recent history of CSR. However, one should also note their limitations and fragility. Fair trade only affects a narrow range of consumer markets; only a small number of retail companies are engaged in fair trade; and there is a recurrent 'intention–behaviour gap' as aggregate data reveal that consumers' real purchasing decisions belie their aspirations to shop responsibly. I dare say that the same would go for many employees who would rather have a job in an organization which was light on CSR than to have no job at all. Still, the vast majority of investment is not accounted for by SRI. It remains to be seen whether the forces which have created limited markets for virtue can expand to have a more general effect. Companies retain a critical role not only in responding to expressions of demand for social criteria in market decisions, but also in shaping products and services that foster and reward those demands.

However, there are also organizations which operate between companies on the one hand and consumers, investors, employees, and society on the other, to promote, manage, and evaluate CSR. Together they constitute an emerging sphere of new governance to which we now turn.

Chapter 5
CSR and new governance

I propose that you ... business leaders ... and we, the United Nations, initiate a Global Compact of shared values and principles, which will give a human face to the global market.

Kofi Annan, UN Secretary-General (1999)

Like Chapter 4, this chapter is also concerned with the institutionalization of CSR, but in this case, institutionalization within systems of societal governance. Nevertheless, the reader will see links between the market-based dynamics covered in Chapter 4 and the governmental, civil society, and business governance initiatives addressed here. CSR emerges both as a means of governing business and as a means of bringing business to wider governance agendas, which is referred to as 'new governance'. CSR features in a range of new governance systems, particularly in the standards and partnerships that institutionalize responsible business behaviour.

New governance refers to ways in which societies are governed. It brings greater governing roles for civil society and business organizations alongside governments. It also complements the exercise of authority with the use of markets and networks as regulatory mechanisms. It brings new models of participation and decision-making in public policies in which consensus-seeking and deliberation are characteristic styles. Much regulation is increasingly of a 'reflexive' nature by which actors regulate themselves in the context of consensually agreed standards. This is designed to avoid inappropriately heavy-handed regulation which is insensitive to companies' and their stakeholders' context and circumstances.

These changes are particularly relevant to understanding the growth of CSR. Over the last few decades, companies have become more responsible for what were considered 'public goods' (i.e. water, energy, communications) hitherto delivered by publicly owned companies for most of the last century. Companies have become increasingly involved in the delivery of major infrastructure projects, and health and education systems, also conventionally associated with governmental delivery. These involvements are not only local and national, but also address social and environmental issues which cross borders, reflecting the international reach of MNCs. Issues of development, climate change, ecological diversity, and demographics are increasingly played out in governance systems with multiple actors, including companies, in new organizations which either reflect or overlap with CSR.

Our review of developments starts with new ways in which business itself defines and manages CSR, through new associations as well as individual companies. It progresses to consider multi-actor organizations in which CSR also gets regulated and organized. Here the focus is upon: UN initiatives and a group of new CSR standards; two organizations which are both standards and partnerships, the Extractive Industries Transparency Initiative (EITI) and the Ethical Trade Initiative (ETI); and a group of resource-specific stewardship councils. Box 13 indicates how CSR fits within new governance.

Business associations

One indicator of increased institutionalization of CSR is that many companies have joined associations to agree and commit to CSR principles, advance CSR agendas, support mutual learning about how to meet peer and societal expectations, and collaborate in specific initiatives (Box 14). This transforms the effect of CSR from being only the sum of many parts to a more coordinated contribution of business resources to societal governance. These associations in turn participate in the range of wider CSR organizations, partnerships, and standards which address an ever wider set of policy issues.

Box14 Continued

Business for Social Responsibility (USA/global 1992; 250+ companies)

CSR Europe (1996; 70+ MNCs and national associations)

ASEAN CSR (2011; ASEAN Foundation and national business associations)

The oldest such association, Business in the Community (BITC) describes itself as standing for responsible business to 'shape a new contract between business and society, in order to secure a fairer society and a more sustainable future'. Box 15 summarizes the services BITC provides to its members.

Box 15 Business in the Community services to members

Advice; Awards and Recognition; Benchmarking; Leadership; Training.

Programmes for sectors (e.g. social enterprises, the arts, the rural sector).

Campaigns (e.g. against requirement for indication of criminal convictions).

Guidance on key issues (i.e. responsible leadership, community, marketplace sustainability, workplace, and employees).

Programmes (e.g. on recruitment of the unemployed; homelessness; diversity issues; market sustainability; sustainable lifestyles; workplace wellness; business transparency).

Frameworks (e.g. for school partnerships, secondments, and volunteering).

There are also international organizations of MNCs which are often more specialized than BITC. The London Benchmarking Group enables members to measure, manage, and report the value and contributions of their community impacts. Founded in the UK in 1994, it now has a global membership of over 300 companies, operating in Australasia, the Czech Republic, Hong Kong/Singapore, Romania, Spain, Poland, and the USA.

The International Business Leaders Forum (IBLF) was founded in 1990 in the UK with the Prince of Wales as it patron. At its peak it had over a hundred company members and combined knowledge development, particularly around the benefits of social partnerships, with more substantive projects in particular regions, such as the former East European and USSR Communist bloc, and issues like sustainable tourism and human rights. It is now being reorganized around several of these individual projects.

The World Business Council for Sustainable Development (WBCSD) was founded in 1992 and consists of the CEOs of over 180 MNCs. It was founded in order to bring a business perspective to the Rio Earth Summit, and retains a special focus on environmental sustainability issues. It too deploys and encourages multi-stakeholder approaches in order to examine the business contribution to sustainability and to develop tools for companies to make such contributions.

In addition to the national and international associations for CSR in general, there are also myriad sector (e.g. Electronics Industry Citizenship Coalition) and issue-based business organizations for CSR (e.g. Business Coalition for HIV Aids).

Multi-actor organizations

Critical to the integration of CSR into new governance is the emergence of numerous multi-actor (also called multi-stakeholder) organizations which either advance CSR or have been adopted to serve CSR. These include international organizations, partnerships, and standards, with business, civil society, and governmental participants. Some of these are designed to regulate CSR and others have been adopted as CSR regulatory sources. In keeping with new governance, and what socio-legal theorists call the 'new accountability', these institutional innovations generate norms and standards of company market behaviour, governance involvement, networks, knowledge development, and accountability systems.

The United Nations CSR initiatives

The interest in the United Nations in CSR is the most conspicuous institutional development of CSR. The centrepiece of this is the UN Global Compact (UNGC) launched in 2000. This followed Secretary-General Kofi Annan's challenge to business leaders at the Davos World Economic Forum to contribute to the governance of the world economy. The initial response was modest (forty business, NGO, labour, and UN agency executives attended the first meeting). However, the UNGC membership has grown and now exceeds 10,000 participants. This includes about 7,000 companies of which nearly 50 per cent employ 250 people or more. The non-business members include: over 400 global NGOs; over 1,000 national NGOs; five international labour organizations; and over 50 national labour organizations. The remaining participants are academics, public sector organizations and cities (see membership by continent in Box 10).

Box 16 introduces the UNGC framework of ten principles addressing four main themes: human rights, labour rights, the environment, and anti-corruption. Business members of the UNGC are expected to integrate these principles into their practices, to support wider UN initiatives, particularly the Millennium Development Goals, and to report annually on their progress in implementation of the principles. Much of the work of the UNGC, often carried out in national chapters (the China and India chapters are among the largest) and partnerships.

Box 16 Ten principles of the UNGC

Human rights (derived from the UN Convention on Human Rights)

1. support and respect the protection of internationally proclaimed human rights;

2. avoid being complicit in human rights abuses;

Labour rights (derived from the International Labor Organization and Rights at Work)

3. uphold the freedom of association and the effective recognition of the right to collective bargaining;

4. elimination of all forms of forced and compulsory labour;

5. the effective abolition of child labour;

6. the elimination of discrimination in respect of employment and occupation;

The environment (derived from the Rio Declaration on Environment and Development)

7. support a precautionary approach to environmental challenges;

8. initiatives to promote greater environmental responsibility;

9. encourage the development and diffusion of environmentally friendly technologies;

Anti-corruption (derived from the UN Convention against Corruption)

10. work against corruption in all its forms, including extortion and bribery.

Whilst the UNGC is sometimes criticized for its lack of coercive capacity, it has more recently shown a readiness to de-list from the UNGC those companies which fail to provide adequate reporting of their social responsibility (about 4,000 to date). Moreover, it has provided a forum for very high level interactions of companies, civil society, and international governmental organizations in core international governance areas.

The UN appointed a special representative for human rights and business, Professor John Ruggie, who worked through extensive multi-actor forums, including legal professionals, to develop, first, a business and human rights framework approved by the UN Human Rights Council (2008). This provided a Framework distinguishing responsibilities among business and governmental actors to protect, respect, and remedy human rights. This was followed by the 2011 Guiding Principles on Business and Human Rights, designed to assist companies implementing the Framework.

The UN Principles for Responsible Investment (2006) result from a collaboration of the UN Environment Programme Finance Initiative and the UNGC. It focuses on environmental, social, and governance issues in investment, and provides guidance to interested finance corporations. Reflecting the new governance style of the other UN CSR initiatives, it was launched following extensive negotiations among investor groups, NGOs, and professionals. The Principles have been signed up to by over 250 asset managers, nearly 800 investment managers, and 180 professional service partners, accounting for about US$35tn assets under management.

International CSR Standards

A plethora of standards has emerged over the last two decades which companies use to design and manage their CSR. Most of these reflect some sort of multi-actor design and governance. Some are more driven by international governmental organizations (e.g. OECD), NGOs (e.g. the Climate Change Group), and organized labour (International Confederation of Trade Unions). Others reflect business origins and direction (e.g. Caux Roundtable, Worldwide Responsible Accredited Production).

Standards can be divided according to whether they are broad-based, or focusing on a particular set of substantive issues like labour rights, the environment, or transparency. They can also be divided according to their operationalization: principles, processes, certification, reporting.

Standards are often about principles (e.g. Caux Roundtable, International Standards Organization (ISO) 26000 on CSR), and are usually designed to assist companies who are unsure about for what and to whom they should be responsible. They tend to be relatively broad in scope, covering human and labour rights, society, the environment, and governance. They usually have developed learning mechanisms to enable signatories to improve their CSR understanding and performance. Although the ISO (1947) usually produces certifiable standards, its social responsibility standard (ISO 26000) remains a guidance document, with the intention of its developing into a certifiable standard. Whilst the standard is available for any organization, most interest has come from corporations.

Process-based standards focus on helping companies to know what they should be doing to ensure that they are operating responsibly. The AccountAbility AA1000 series addresses issues affecting governance, business models, and organizational strategy, as well as sustainability assurance and stakeholder engagement.

Some standards provide a means of certification. The SA 8000 standard, focusing on employment practices and free collective action, was launched in 1997 by the US Social Accountability International. The standard is currently certified in over 3,000 companies employing nearly two million workers in over seventy countries. The Fair Labor Association (FLA) offers a set of ten labour and human rights-based principles that members, mainly in the consumer product industries sign up to, conformance with which is monitored by the FLA. The ISO 14000 code has been employed by companies concerned with their environmental impacts.

The most well-known reporting standard is the Global Reporting Initiative (GRI) which aims to improve organizations' accountability for standards of sustainability. The GRI is a network of user organizations guided by a Board of Directors, a Stakeholder Council, and a Technical Advisory Committee, all of which reflect international, multi-stakeholder principles. It provides a comprehensive and certifiable framework for sustainability reporting. Although the full framework is used only in about 1,000 organizations per year, these include leading corporations, including about 75 per cent of the Fortune Global 250. Moreover, thousands of companies use elements of the framework in their UNGC corporate communications, for example. The GRI has been recognized by other governmental organizations, including the G8, as the international authority on sustainability reporting, and is specifically referenced in the Danish and Swedish reporting regulations.

The Extractive Industries Transparency Initiative

The Extractive Industries Transparency Initiative (EITI) offers a framework for extractive industry companies to account for their taxation and other payments made to host country governments. This provides accountability not only of themselves but also of the respective governments. The EITI was launched by UK Prime Minister, Tony Blair, in 2002. It was initially coordinated and funded by the UK government but its international secretariat is now in Oslo. About 50 per cent of the budget is covered by governments and development agencies and the remainder by the investor and extractive companies themselves.

The EITI Standard (originally 'principles') has been adopted by thirty-seven countries and is supported by over eighty oil, gas, and mining companies. These governments and companies each report relevant payments which are verified and reported by the EITI. Over eighty global investment institutions, responsible for more than US$19tn investment have signed the Investors Statement on Transparency in the Extractives Sector, which is also crucial given that the sector is so capital intensive. Finally, the EITI is partnered by another dozen key governance institutions, such as development agencies, international financial institutions, international mining associations, and inter-governmental organizations.

The Ethical Trading Initiative

The Ethical Trading Initiative (ETI) was also launched by the UK government following informal discussions with companies, NGOs, and trade unions who then formed an alliance committed to transparency in workers' rights in agricultural and manufacturing supply chains. There are over seventy member corporations with a combined turnover of over £166bn and supply chains of 10 million workers. Civil society members include trade unions, representing about 160 million workers, and NGOs, such as Oxfam, CAFOD, Fairtrade Foundation, and Save the Children. The UK government retains observer status on the ETI Board, provides some core funding and deploys the organizational resources of its regional and country offices.

Member companies sign up to a base code and report annually on their sourcing operations against this code. Training courses are provided to support member and non-member companies. Random inspections are made by civil society organizations on the basis of which the ETI has requested suppliers to take more than 133,000 actions to improve workers' conditions. The ETI retains the right to terminate or suspend the membership of companies failing to comply.

The ETI has contributed to the wider institutionalization of CSR having attracted non-UK company members and having been adopted by Danish and Norwegian counterparts. In 2013, the Nordic Council of Ministers launched the Nordic Strategy on Corporate Social Responsibility and commissioned the Danish and Norwegian ETIs to run the initiative on global value chains and to facilitate similar organizations in Finland, Sweden, and Iceland. Following the Rana Plaza collapse in Bangladesh (2013), the UK, Danish, and Norwegian ETIs developed an ETI programme on Garments from Bangladesh to improve labour rights, and health and safety which was conditional upon the Bangladesh government increasing minimum wages and removing obstacles to trade union formation.

Stewardship Councils

Another feature of CSR in new governance is the emergence of Stewardship Councils, which combine expert assessment of the sustainable sourcing of a natural resource with certification and branding opportunities for companies complying with the standards.

The Forest Stewardship Council launched in 1993 reflecting the triple bottom line approach in its mission statement ('Environmentally Appropriate; Socially Beneficial; Economically Viable') and in its governance design. The General Assembly is made up of North and South members representing environmental, social, and economic organizations. By 2011, it had issued over 20,000 'chain of custody' certificates to sourcing companies and 1,000 'forest management certificates'. The FSC logo is now used by companies to demonstrate their CSR, while numerous public bodies use FSC certification in their public procurement policies.

The Marine Stewardship Council was launched in 1999 following a CSR-type partnership between Unilever and the World Wildlife

Fund for Nature designed to investigate and address the world's depleting fish stocks. The MSC, now independent of Unilever, certifies about 200 fisheries, with another hundred in the certification process, representing over 10 per cent of the world's wild fish stocks. Over 22,000 seafood products are traceable to these fisheries, and use the MSC logo. The MSC also certifies restaurants in about ten countries, including Australia, South Africa, UK, and USA.

Unilever has followed this up with the recent launch of its Sustainable Agriculture Code and the first product to promote a sustainable ingredient was Knorr soups and sustainable tomatoes. Unilever also uses external partners for ensuring the stewardship of other products, including the Rainforest Alliance for sustainable cocoa and vanilla beans, and Green Palm Certificates for palm oil.

The institutionalization of CSR: a summary

The integration of social criteria into market transactions and the role of business in new governance mechanisms have both contributed to the remarkable institutionalization of CSR (Boxes 12 and 13 capture these dynamics). In other words, CSR is becoming part of business as usual and it is a more regular feature of societal governance.

As a result CSR is not only about corporate discretion but about company choices in a more tangible context of social regulation and opportunity. From a societal perspective, business is more widely regarded as having social responsibilities as well as bringing distinctive capacities for societal governance. A variety of mechanisms now expand the social gaze on the impacts of companies. Companies are more widely recognized as being able to bring distinctive resources of knowledge and networks, and capacity for innovation and flexibility to governance challenges.

They also bring international reach such that they are able to address cross-border governance challenges.

In one sense, though, the growth of these new CSR systems poses a different set of challenges for companies: which standard to adopt, or which partnership to join, and why? More generally the very multiplicity of these innovations can be confusing not only for companies but also for their suppliers and customers. As a result companies spend a lot of time and other resources thinking about reporting and systematizing their responsibilities, rather than managing them. Perhaps this is an inevitable stage, and some rationalization and integration of the systems will emerge?

Moreover, it is striking that few of the CSR systems we have noted are concerned with the evaluation of companies' social impact, which was, after all, the whole point of CSR. On which note, we turn to criticisms of CSR.

Chapter 6
Critical perspectives

*It's about politics and business. But it's not about democracy
and markets.*

Australian taxi driver (2013)

Notwithstanding the story of CSR growth among companies,
countries, markets, and new organizations, controversies have
raged about CSR from outside and even among its adherents. CSR
is often perceived as not adequately addressing key issues held
dear by the respective critics: that CSR is gender blind; that it has
been associated with the exploitation of indigenous people; that it
is complicit with oppressive governments, for example. These
perspectives tend to be about selected outcomes rather than
formed on the basis of a systematic critique of CSR's rationale.

This chapter focuses on two more systemic critiques, which argue
that CSR is fundamentally undesirable or impossible. Both
critiques are presented and then their respective main lines of
attack are responded to from a CSR perspective. First, there is the
view associated with Milton Friedman which sees CSR as being
contrary to the core purpose of business; as representing
unaccountable management excess at the expense of
shareholders; and as undermining democratic accountability for
public affairs. Secondly, there is the anti-corporate perspective,
usually associated with critics of capitalism more generally. This

view sees CSR as an extension of, and even a fig-leaf for, the underlying problems of capitalism and of corporations therein. Some versions of this second critique share Friedman's preference for government and democratic processes, rather than CSR, as a means of resolving social problems. Notwithstanding my rebuttal of key elements of both critiques of CSR, there is a sense in which CSR is necessarily contested, even among its adherents, on which theme the chapter concludes.

The business of business is business

One of the most cited texts in CSR literature is Milton Friedman's 1970 essay, 'The social responsibility of business is to increase its profits'. This is surprising given Friedman's antipathy to CSR and given that the essay appeared in the *New York Times Magazine*. The article succinctly reflects views that Friedman had expressed in other published works and in his more general public engagement on the social contribution of markets and on the proper responsibilities of managers.

Friedman had already established himself as a champion of neo-liberalism and opponent of Keynesian economic policy, and was a future Nobel Prize-winner for Economic Sciences (1976). He was alarmed by CSR and saw it as a fundamental threat to capitalism. This is illustrated by his view that the CSR advocates were 'preaching pure and unadulterated socialism' which, for Friedman, was about as bad as it could get. He asserted that:

> There is one and only one social responsibility of business—to use its resources and engage in activities designed to increase its profits so long as its stays within the rules of the game.

Friedman added that this should be in accordance with 'customary ethics'. His argument was premised on the view that, unless they were told otherwise, managers' primary duty is to maximize profits for the company owners; by which he meant shareholders. This was on the immediate grounds of ethics and accountability, but also because Friedman adhered to Adam Smith's view that markets offer an 'invisible' mechanism for creating employment, providing goods and services to customers at acceptable prices as well as rewarding investors. Thus, attention to markets best serves managers, shareholders, and society.

Friedman caricatured managers' inclination to pursue CSR as being about indulging their pet social projects by using other people's (i.e. shareholders') money to those ends. Instead, he argued, socially motivated managers should devote their own resources to these causes in their own time (e.g. through charities) and they should devote their working time to the interests of shareholders on whose behalf they are employed.

Moreover, Friedman mounted another accountability argument against CSR, contending that democratically elected representatives, not business managers, are accountable for public affairs. Finally, he added a competency argument, that business managers have no expertise in matters of public policy, but that elected representatives and appointed officials have appropriate training and experience.

Friedman on CSR assessed

The social responsibility and business dichotomy

In part Friedman's preference for a dichotomy between social responsibility (i.e. that which he sees as the governmental sphere) and business is predicated on his assumptions that markets, if left to their own devices, will function to maximize social as well as economic benefits. There is a variety of views among CSR writers and practitioners about the virtues of markets. However, there is a general view that markets are capable of serving society, but can also be contorted and exploited. First, advocates would point to the information asymmetries that much CSR is designed to address through standards and transparency initiatives. Secondly, they would see the problems of negative social and environmental externalities of companies in markets, again which CSR is designed to address. In other words, if markets worked as Adam Smith had envisaged, then we would not need CSR!

What is more, Friedman did not consider the sorts of value to companies of the investments in responsible business that we have observed around social, political and environmental risk, efficiency, innovation and the pursuit of new markets (Chapters 2 and 4). He did not anticipate CSR developing into ways of doing business responsibly, but simply regarded it as a cost. He did not appear to consider that managers and shareholders might be capable of dispassionately identifying ways in which CSR might serve profit-making.

This gap is surprising given that Friedman, in what seems like a throw-away line, identifies a business benefit from a social investment. Friedman concedes that a company might invest in community amenities in order to win the loyalty of the workforce and thereby increase productivity and reduce shirking and pilfering. In this somewhat cynical variant of the employee motivation for CSR, Friedman observes that 'to call this responsibility would be fraudulent': it is an investment.

Taking this semantic refuge suggests that Friedman was unaware of, or preferred to ignore, the long-held view in the corporate philanthropy and CSR literature, that social investments could secure community legitimacy and thereby inform employee loyalty and motivation. Moreover, having made this single insight into the possible business benefits of social performance, he was unable to extend this logic to wider opportunities for a business case for CSR.

More broadly, it is striking how many corporate leaders now attest to the business benefits of CSR: can they all be guilty of what Friedman called 'socialism' or 'mere window-dressing'?

A corporate governance hijack?

We now turn to Friedman's corporate governance argument that managers should simply assume that shareholders want them to make as much profit as possible, and that this is what managers should prioritize. This view has subsequently been popularized in the form of the 'agent–principal' relationship, which assumes that the manager is the agent of the principal, the shareholders. This view has acquired almost theological status in management education in large part because of the impact of business academics Jensen and Meckling, whose term 'agency theory' encapsulates these views. Outside business schools, the agent–principal relationship was popularized by Jack Welch, CEO of General Electric, who argued that shareholder profits are the principal measure of a firm's success.

Whilst Friedman and his disciples make much of the rights of shareholders as 'owners', the principle of the corporation having distinct legal identity from its shareholders has been long established in corporate law. Thus the concept of ownership is rather less straightforward than in privately owned companies. In short, the company owns its assets.

Manifestly, however, shareholders do and should count: the power of SRI is precisely because shareholders have influence. Shareholder meetings and board members appointed by shareholders are clearly pivotal in the appointments of CEOs and other executives; in their remuneration; in decisions about acquisitions or stock offerings; and in the general directions that corporations take. Although they might acquire finance by other means, such as loans or the accumulation of profits, publicly listed corporations depend on shareholding for their viability.

But questions remain about the exclusivity of the manager–shareholder relationship. Even in the 'canon' of Anglo-American corporate governance, Berle and Means refer to managers' capacity to balance community claims on the company and to assign resources accordingly. Anglo-American corporate governance requires managers to act 'for the company' and the 2006 UK Companies Act Amendment added 'and the benefits of its members as a whole'. Whilst US courts would find a management mission that 'seeks not to maximize the economic value of a for-profit...corporation for the benefit of its stockholders' incompatible with fiduciary duty, they nonetheless accept that companies should play a social role, often using the phrase 'high obligations'. UK Courts have upheld the principle of corporate philanthropy for nearly a century. Moreover, other branches of Anglo-American law recognize interests other than those of the owners, most obviously in cases of bankruptcy or insolvency laws where the rights of creditors, employees, and pensioners are also recognized. Most non-Anglo-American corporate governance specifies the interests of other constituents or stakeholders rather than shareholders alone.

Interestingly, following the global financial crisis of 2007, Jack Welch, who, in addition to his leadership of GE, was also author of the 'Welch Way', which prioritized productivity, efficiency, and profitability, reconsidered his position: 'On the face of it, shareholder value is the dumbest idea in the world. Shareholder value is a result, not a strategy...your main constituencies are your employees, your customers and your products.'

However, the agent–principal argument and the implied assumption that the principals' priority is profit-maximization continues to be used against CSR. It has a basic appeal notwithstanding the caveats in corporate governance and jurisprudence. Although the ethical investment movement was in its infancy when Friedman was writing, this has subsequently grown. With it have grown both the view of many shareholders that CSR can be a sensible investment in their companies' competitiveness and the mainstreaming of social and environmental risk.

The public affairs and business dichotomy

Friedman's argument that public affairs should be left to politicians and public officials implies that the political and the business spheres are, and should be, mutually exclusive. It is curious that, CSR apart, Friedman seemed unaware of the involvement of corporations in American political life of his time. Corporations and industry associations are well known for their involvement in electoral, congressional, and judicial politics given their interests in the effects of such policy issues as tariffs and quotas; public expenditure on defence; subsidies in agriculture and industry; fiscal and monetary strategies; rules about environmental pollution; energy choices; and employment rights.

Whilst these roles are sometimes controversial (e.g. Citizens United vs Federal Election Commission, USA, 2010; Australian mining industry campaign against the carbon tax), the principle of business political involvement is broadly legitimized in democratic capitalism, and certainly in the USA. In some European systems, business associations contribute to public policy-making through neo-corporatist institutional structures. This suggests that in order to substantiate the view that CSR offends a business–public affairs dichotomy, Friedmanites need to demonstrate that CSR distinctively subverts the political sphere.

Certainly Friedman's anxieties about the negative—even corrupting—possibilities of business and government relations would be understood from a CSR standpoint. But wishing away the complexity into imagined dichotomized spheres hardly helps (see Chapter 7).

Friedman's claims about the distinctive suitability of democratic government for accountability are paradoxical in view of Friedman's wider critique of government for the lack of accountable governance in social welfare. Friedman is renowned for pointing to the self-serving nature of bureaucrats and politicians and the deleterious implications of their self-interest for the public good. However, Friedman's claim here that business managers are essentially self-interested and that elected representatives and public officials are not is curious. Presumably, managers in either sector may be self-interested.

This brings us to the fact that in 1970—like today—most people in the world lived under non-democratic systems of government, to which Friedman appears to have given no thought. It is strange that Friedman should not have considered mechanisms for accountability for corporations, including US ones, operating in non-democratic societies.

From a CSR perspective democratic accountability is to be welcomed in societal governance, but this is hardly pitted against corporate accountability. The former provides the opportunity for polity-wide mandates and periodic opportunities to hold governments to account. Yet corporate executives are accountable in different ways. They are vulnerable to dismissal and are required to account for themselves at annual general meetings. They are required to make annual, and even quarterly, reports on their financial—and now environmental, social, and governance—progress and impacts. Some CSR innovations like the EITI enhance governmental accountability, particularly in the non-democratic world, and government regulations, such as ESG reporting requirements, can improve business accountability). More broadly, we have seen the interrelationship, rather than dichotomy, of business and government (and civil society) capacities and accountability systems in CSR and new governance (Chapter 5).

Then and now

Since Friedman wrote this essay, business accountability appears to have increased as a result of both CSR and an associated movement for wider environmental, social, and governance accountability. As we have seen in earlier chapters, innovations, such as external social impact evaluations (e.g. by SRI analysts), systems for stakeholder involvement, and business membership of multi-actor new governance institutions, appear to have set accountability standards way beyond those in operation in 1970.

Turning to the argument that managers may not have the requisite expertise to address social problems, Friedman suggests that corporations might unleash managers who are amateurs in the worlds of education, the natural environment, and human rights. Yet one of the most interesting recent CSR trends is how corporations work with experts from government, civil society, and professions to develop and manage their CSR, as well as to thereby secure their legitimacy.

Finally, the increase in globalization since 1970 has brought to light many more accountability issues for corporations than anyone in 1970 might have anticipated. In other words, the national laws and customary ethics on which Friedman relies for moral steering of business, may have less purchase in securing responsible business, including in US companies, than he expected. Accordingly it is fair to conclude that Friedman could not have anticipated the CSR agendas now facing US corporations, particularly, nor the international institutionalization of CSR in supply chains emanating from undemocratic societies.

Friedman's standard bearers

Notwithstanding the limitations of Friedman's case against CSR, his standard-bearers persist, particularly in attesting to the primacy of the 'agent–principal' relationship, the costs for business of the substitution of goals that they perceive in adopting CSR, the supremacy of markets for delivering social benefits, as well as the superiority of government as a source of enforceable regulation.

The Economist magazine has been a forthright adherent of Friedman's view though it has conceded some of the CSR claims. It persists with some of Friedman's assumptions such as that legal and ethical 'selfish' profit-making is itself good for company stakeholders and the social and economic deficiencies of governments. There is also a gentle implied criticism of those who 'intone' Friedman's argument. *The Economist* has attested to the value of companies making community investments in hard times from a legitimacy perspective, and concurred that CSR can enrich the companies and society. It has also concluded that CSR 'has won the battle of ideas'; has become mainstreamed into company strategy; is no longer a 'do-gooding sideshow'; and is 'evolving and becoming a little less flaky'. However it often opines that CSR could still be better managed, by which it means better aligned with companies' overall strategy. We now turn to the second critical perspective on CSR.

The business of business is anti-social

This set of critiques is ostensibly antithetical to that of Friedman in that its mainsprings are anti-capitalist, though we will find some agreement with aspects of the Friedmanite view that may be unsettling to both sides! This perspective has not had the benefit of such a concise and integrated adumbration as Friedman's and, accordingly, it is rather more heterogeneous. The voices include those from the academy (e.g. the 'critical management field'), critical NGOs, and critical scrutinizers of business within the media: the modern-day 'muckrakers'.

The arguments can be reconstructed as suggesting that: corporations and executives are self-interested and unsociable; CSR covers over unseemly profit-making, enabling negative social impacts of business to go unregulated; CSR undermines democratic accountability; and it is part of 'corporate takeover' of the social and the political spheres. For some of the critics, governments are the preferred means of addressing social issues.

Corporations and managers are self-interested and unsociable

The view that corporations and their managers are self-interested is a common basis for critique of CSR. Whereas Adam Smith sees self-interest as a virtue in a market setting, the critics regard CSR as self-evidently anti-social because corporations are self-interested and, thereby, anti-social. Thus CSR is, by dint of its corporate origins, ill-suited to social responsibility. Others, with Marx, view self-interest as axiomatic in the logic of capitalism and thus, with the best will in the world, corporations are unable to offer any long-term social benefit and to do so would risk their own competiveness, profitability, and survival.

Joel Bakan's book and film, *The Corporation*, present the idea of the corporation as a psychopath. It suggests that corporate scandals are not just the result of 'a few bad apples', which was President George W. Bush's response to the Enron scandal. Rather they result from the corporation not only being the pre-eminent institution but also one that by design was bent on self-interest. Despite being the creation of governments through regulation, they are in Judge Brandeis's 1930 analogy like 'Frankenstein's monster'. Rather than being loyal or subservient to their creators, they overpower them.

The analysis of corporate anti-sociability and the metaphor of the psychopath is also applied at the level of corporate leaders by some critics. George Monbiot, for example, argues that corporate leaders acquire their positions as a result either of elite advantages they inherit or of ruthless exploitation of others. He suggests that senior managers and CEOs bear remarkably similar character traits to psychopathic criminals—egocentrism, a sense of entitlement, exploitation of others, and a lack of empathy. Thus, for Monbiot, team-playing and productivity have been devalued and corporations have encouraged an unproductive rentier class which is over-rewarded. Its focus is not upon wealth creation but on wealth accumulation. Joseph Stiglitz, another Economics Nobel Prize-winner, extends this critique by pointing to the excessive inequality that has resulted from the way in which corporate leadership behaviour undermines community. This raises the question as to how companies can be socially responsible if they are led by such people?

CSR is a fig leaf for unsociability

In this light it is clear why many contemporary critics regard CSR as a facade for the real face of capitalism, corporations, and corporate leaders. Echoing Friedman's term 'window-dressing', they describe CSR as 'green-washing' or 'blue-washing'. It distracts society from the underlying acquisitive and anti-social nature of corporations, and thus from serious social scrutiny. These critics point to the ways in which CSR is often used for marketing purposes, so as to present a human and caring face of business, one that is gentle with nature and reliable.

Rather than embracing social and environmental issues whole-heartedly, this view sees CSR as a means of corporate cooptation of social issues. This gives the appearance of social solidarity enabling corporations to temper the force of the radicalism behind the social agendas. One critic observes that as corporations appear to embrace gender issues: 'feminist values have become diluted and selectively incorporated to legitimize and sustain institutionalized injustices.' Other critics complain that CSR can yield company benefits through exploitation of involvement in social issues. They point to the benefits that retailers obtain from social marketing, for example, where a company supports a social cause by bringing its marketing and other resources to bear, and thereby increases its own profits.

More generally, CSR is regarded as a means by which social issues get marketized, as opposed to markets getting socialized. Thus, individuals and organizations who really want to influence international development agendas, for example, are distracted from political projects and campaigns by engagement with CSR.

Instead their energies are channelled into 'strategies of consumption', as some critics depict the fair trade movement and ethical trade initiatives. CSR therefore compounds the underlying structure of the exploitative and unequal international political economy.

CSR side-steps the key business impacts on society

It would follow from the previous points that because of the distractions of CSR, the socially and environmentally destructive impacts of business go less noticed, get less politicized, and go unregulated or inappropriately regulated.

This point about the real social impacts of corporations being eclipsed by CSR can be illustrated with reference to the role of the banks in recent revelations of irresponsibility. Many of the 'high street' banks have acquired reputations for their sociability. In some cases this reflects legacies of the company founders, such as Barclays whose Quaker founders and long-time company leaders prided themselves on their responsibility and probity. Most major banks had employed CSR staff and produced CSR reports attesting to their positive impacts. The Royal Bank of Scotland had won community involvement awards for the way its community policies were designed to spread financial literacy to sections of the population excluded from the benefits of banking and, more broadly.

Yet these policies distracted from what is now recognized as socially irresponsible lending to borrowers who were proved all too vulnerable to national and individual changes in economic circumstances. More fundamentally, they distracted from the logics of financial packages devised by banks that systematically over-valued assets and led to the 2007 crash. The critics of CSR can point to numerous examples of irresponsibility out of the spotlight coinciding with accolades and claims about responsibility under the spotlight.

CSR and the 'corporate takeover'

CSR is not only criticized for enabling corporations to hide their real intent and purpose, or to cynically benefit from thin marketing gestures. More fundamentally, it is argued that CSR constitutes a key element in the corporate takeover of the social and political spheres. Noam Chomsky, linguist, 'rebel without a pause', and long-time critic of business and of corporate responsibility, describes corporations as taking over government and others refer to the 'marketization of the political'.

This view has a forerunner in the critique that corporations have always ruled by indirect and invisible means. This is reflected in the view that, by dint of their size and resources, corporations have special power. This can include the implied threat that corporations have over governments of the ability to withdraw capital from a country whose regulatory framework impairs profit-maximizing. In this light, societies and governments become obsequious to, and complicit with, the interests of corporations.

Another version goes that through marketing, corporations can shape our tastes and thus our expenditures and consumption. Critics point to the way in which corporations have encouraged consumption of products in the full knowledge that this increases health risks to their customers.

CSR undermines democratic accountability

Whilst some CSR critics see democratic accountability as a facade under capitalism, for others this is not inevitably the case. There is a critical view which retains confidence in the possibilities of democratic, accountable government either to simply set rules which require greater levels of business responsibility or to deliver public policies more purposefully.

A prominent adherent to the anti-CSR, pro-government view is Robert Reich, formerly President Clinton's Secretary for Labor. He recently revised earlier enthusiasm for CSR, concurring with Friedman by arguing that CSR is a side-show, diverting attention from serious problems, and that it is an unaccountable expenditure of other people's money. He concluded by advocating that government should set the rules to ensure the corporations do not act irresponsibly regarding environmental pollution and human rights, for example.

Anti-capitalist CSR critiques in perspective

Responses from the CSR quarter to these anti-corporate criticisms vary. For those who regard CSR as a fulfilment of capitalism as a responsive mechanism, there will be little sympathy. Others who take the view that CSR moderates the anti-social impacts of capitalism will have some sympathy with some of the anti-capitalist critiques without agreeing with remedies implied or proposed. They will stress the ways in which CSR can change capitalism, particularly in remedying information asymmetries, and in identifying and addressing corporations' negative social and environmental impacts.

Markets, self-interest, and unsociability

CSR advocates are unlikely to accept the view that markets are *intrinsically* socially destructive any more than they would accept Friedman's premise that unfettered markets will maximize social welfare. They tend to see the operation of markets not in absolute but in contingent terms. Thus it might be readily conceded that there are socially perverse elements of capitalism (e.g. 'the race to the bottom'). But its advocates would see CSR as a propitious means of eliminating the negative. They would also point to the ways in which corporations respond to and reflect investor and consumer pressure. CSR would be posited as another opportunity to bring in the social, as illustrated in our discussion of the socialization of markets (Chapter 5).

CSR and corporate power

Underlying most of the anti-corporate bases for CSR critiques is usually an idea of corporate power. In particular, this view presumes that power is not subject to the constraints of markets, society, or even regulators. Certainly, CSR advocates recognize corporate power. This is both why corporations need to be held accountable and why they can bring distinctive resources and opportunities propitious for social purposes.

As with their views on markets, CSR advocates see nothing inevitable or fundamentally subversive about this power. Nor yet would they see this power as necessarily greater than that of governments or society. Their point would be that power is contingent, and that appropriate mechanisms need to be put in place (be they market-, government-, or society-based). These mechanisms would encourage CSR innovators; cajole the laggards; and police the unsociable corporations.

CSR opinions are divided on the critique that CSR is too often defined by the corporations and not by society. For some this would be core to their understandings of CSR and entirely desirable: CSR is about corporate discretion. Others might concede that this was true fifty years ago, but that since the 1990s, CSR has become much more a matter of social regulation of business, as reflected in CSR's changing dynamics, scope, and institutionalization.

CSR as marketing in disguise

Leaving aside the wanton abuse of CSR symbols and connotations, there is likely to be some sympathy with the view that CSR can be 'spun' and thereby mask irresponsibility. It may be inevitable that positive, or evaluative, normative terms get abused: witness the adoption of the word 'democratic' in the national names of manifestly undemocratic places! Moreover, the adoption of the language of social responsibility in business, even by those who do so cynically, may even be considered as something of an advance.

It implies that corporations are aware that this is what society or particular stakeholders expect, and that they may benefit from being seen to be sociable.

Feminists have noted that the casual or cynical use of feminist rhetoric, including by companies, can actually offer them a resource: the inference is that the corporations have to live up to their words, be it about gender equality or CSR, or suffer the opprobrium of being labelled hypocritical. It is interesting to see how certain corporations which have invested in their reputation for CSR are keen to be seen to be acting consistently when subjected to critique, as can be observed in Nike's successive improvements in its supply chain labour standards. Others are embarrassed when hypocrisy is suggested; thus Starbucks offered the UK Inland Revenue Department an *ex gratia* payment in lieu of the corporate taxation it had avoided.

In short, CSR advocates who share the anti-corporate disquiet about inappropriate CSR marketing will tend to suggest that the pursuit of transparency and accountability, core CSR concerns, will inhibit or punish such irresponsible behaviour.

A more regulated alternative?

Most CSR adherents would concur that regulations can be most welcome in order to enable corporations to be clearly guided about core social expectations and to enable the punishment of free-riders. As we have seen, the distinctions between CSR as an unregulated phenomenon on the one hand, and the governmental regulation of business have become more blurred. Government regulation now overlaps with, draws upon, and encourages CSR.

Generally, speaking CSR advocates sit somewhere between Friedmanite and anti-capitalist criticisms, rejecting both sets of deductive logics and their respective implications for the sociability and accountability of markets. Indeed, many in the CSR camp would go further and argue that CSR provides mechanisms to address the very global governance gaps that many in the anti-corporate camp attribute to the role of corporations in globalization.

In essence, CSR is a reformist project which seeks improvement of the systems we have rather than theory-led change. We have seen that markets can serve the social aspirations of consumers and investors with appropriate attention to information and certified labelling. We have also seen how CSR is melding into new governance organizations and practices. In Chapter 7 we reflect further on limitations in CSR identified in the anti-corporate critiques.

CSR as essentially contested

Corporate Social Responsibility

The topic of critiques of CSR cannot be left without noting that CSR is contested not only by its critics, but also among those who embrace it. But disagreement among adherents of evaluative concepts is not unusual. This is because adherents disagree about precisely which values are absolutely vital, without which the concept would not exist, even though they agree on the existence and the value of, in this case, CSR. Thus when CSR takes a new turn there are some who will regard this as incompatible with CSR's core meaning.

Perhaps the two most important areas of disagreement and difficulty concern CSR's relationship with profit-making and with government, reflecting the Friedmanite and anti-corporate perspectives. The first area of dispute is over the status of 'the business case for CSR'. While many see it as 'good business', others would argue that if CSR does not involve a cost to business, then why would it be called 'responsibility'? The second involves the relationship of CSR with government policies or initiatives. Whereas some see adherence to and partnership with government as a key indicator of CSR, others would say that this is simply compliance or strategic positioning, and not CSR.

These dichotomies can be unrealistic and unhelpful. With respect to the business case issue, it is reasonable to expect that many CSR ventures would be rewarded by society, for example through consumer, employee, or investor choices, even though their motivation may also be more intrinsically around 'doing the right thing'. In this respect CSR may perhaps be compared with the concept of 'social capital' in which, through membership of social networks, individuals gain long-run benefits as a result of being trusted. The enthusiasts of social capital are not cynical about the rewards afforded to those who invest in it by being generous and cooperative. No more so should there be face-value cynicism simply because a company is rewarded for its CSR.

With respect to the issue of the CSR and government relationship, it is unrealistic to see CSR as an alternative to government. In reality, CSR, like all business ventures, is embedded in contexts of complementary provision by other actors, primarily governments, but also families, communities, and charities. Moreover, much public policy and even regulation still permits a high degree of business choice about whether and how to conform or participate. Thus, except in cases where regulation specifies precisely the requirements of the law and punishments for non-compliance, a high degree of corporate discretion remains within business and society relations, notwithstanding governmental purpose therein. This discretion enables corporations to choose CSR albeit in an environment framed by regulations. Indeed this has been the case for all charitable contributions of individuals and businesses alike in Anglo-American jurisdictions since the Charitable Uses Act of 1601!

Thus, the answer to the question 'what responsibility is entailed in CSR?' is simply 'it depends', as we also saw in Chapter 3. And this is one of the reasons why CSR can be frustrating to companies who are unsure of their responsibilities as well as to those who see business as operating most efficiently and socially beneficially when it is unencumbered by concerns about its social responsibilities.

Chapter 7
Prospects and reflections

When the market fails to achieve an optimal state, society
will, to some extent at least recognize the gap and non-mar-
ket institutions will arise attempting to bridge it.
Kenneth Arrow, Economics Nobel Prize-winner (1963)

It could be argued that CSR, particularly as it has been
institutionalized in the last decade, is a realization of Kenneth
Arrow's expectation that non-market institutions will compensate
for the social shortcomings of markets. We have seen how markets
have been socialized and that CSR features in new forms of
relatively socially inclusive governance. Conversely, with the
recent litany of financial corporations' failings alone, it could be
argued that CSR has failed to sufficiently socialize business and
corporations in particular. Accordingly, questions arise as to
whether and how CSR should develop, and whether other
non-market institutions can and should interpose?

Clues to CSR's future are often confusing. For example, a recent
MORI poll found that most companies see their corporate
responsibility as becoming more 'embedded' in the next five years.
Yet only one-third of CEOs surveyed by Accenture thought that
the global economy is on track to meet the demands of a growing
population in the context of environmental and resource
constraints.

Despite the growing significance of non-market institutions for framing CSR, it remains a 'business-oriented' phenomenon and thus business circumstances will be critical to CSR futures. At an individual business level, these circumstances can depend on numerous factors, most obviously, leadership, commercial fortunes, social impacts, and stakeholder relations. We first consider broader factors of economic, business, and environmental and social futures. Then we turn to the societal expectations of business, in particular the issue of extending CSR to companies' political engagement.

Economic futures

A key consideration for CSR prospects is economic growth, be it fast or slow, global or regional, or even local. Whilst none of these economic futures is in essence more or less compatible with CSR, their overall effects may well shape its form and spread. The nature of economic growth and its geographical coverage and linkages are likely to inform the types of businesses that will dominate markets, as well as their social, economic, environmental, and political impacts.

Fast economic growth is likely to be associated with greater emphasis on waste and increased consumption of scarce natural resources. These are likely to be critical for business impacts on climate change, and on the availability and distribution of food and water, for example. Business may also become more embroiled in domestic political issues about meeting skill needs, provoking debates about migrant labour versus training domestic labour. This scenario is likely to see CSR being more easily supported with financial resources associated with increased profits.

Slow economic growth is likely to be associated with increased levels of unemployment and associated poverty, and personal and national debt. These would make for CSR agendas around managing with less, and the socio-economic survival of exposed communities. In these circumstances, companies may well see CSR as vital to their own legitimacy, as business may be described as part of the problem that led to the downturn in the first place, just asthe banks are blamed following the 2007 crisis. There may be disincentives for investing in cleaner technologies and consuming renewable energy, for example.

Increased globalization is likely to see the relative growth of the transport and communications industries, which would support, among other things, the increased movement and distribution of resources, services, and products. This would bring a host of CSR issues associated with social, environmental, and economic costs and benefits. For example, energy price rises associated with global growth may spur innovation for renewable energies and greener production systems.

There are also the possible interactive effects of globalization and more regional and local business patterns. For example, wage growth and greater regulation in less developed countries may prompt Western country MNCs to reinvest in supply chains closer to home. This may also enable them to reduce association with supply chain scandals such as the recent Bangladesh factory disasters as announced by two Australian retail companies. Alternatively, a retailer which continues to source from Bangladesh may need to change its supply chain business models (e.g. the use of independent buyers). If these changes entailed increased costs, a company may also need to manage a responsible consumption CSR policy to tolerate price increases resulting from higher wages, lower working hours, and greater health and safety in developing country supply chains.

Business futures

Future CSR may also be shaped by developments in sources of finance and broad business models. One effect of the financial crisis has been the relative growth of two sources of business finance not conventionally associated with CSR: sovereign wealth funds (SWFs) and private equity. Together these account for over 10 per cent of the US$80tn funds under management.

The top thirty SWFs alone are valued at about US$6tn. Most large SWFs are from non-democratic systems like Abu Dhabi, China, Saudi Arabia, Kuwait, and Russia. They have acquired shares in Western business in infrastructure (e.g. London's Gatwick and Heathrow Airports; Thames Water), communications (e.g. Royal Mail), and insurance and banking (e.g. Barclays, UBS, Credit Suisse). Some of these acquisitions have provoked national security anxieties, particularly in the USA. Due to their lack of transparency, little is known about the CSR commitments of most big SWFs other than the Norway Government Pension Fund. Most SWFs are associated with countries known for their antipathy to human rights and gender equality, for example. However, SWFs' entry into Western markets has required them to improve their financial transparency and in many cases this also entails them in social accountability requirements.

The value of private equity is necessarily hard to calculate, but its estimated value is about US$3tn. Likewise the attitude of private equity to CSR is difficult to evaluate. Sceptics can point to the association of private equity with asset-stripping in the 1980s and to recent estimates that fewer than 15 per cent of private equity groups calculate the value generated through a company's environmental, social and governance programmes. However, if private equity owners aim to prepare companies for future flotation, they may need to invest in the responsible and sustainable attributes that potential buyers may increasingly consider obligatory.

In the UK about 1,000 companies per year receive some sort of private equity finance, and these include two historic UK CSR icons. Boots the Chemist appears if anything to be more transparent about its CSR since it was bought out, but it has moved its HQ to Switzerland thereby avoiding UK corporation tax. The 70 per cent private equity ownership of the Cooperative Bank has brought the prospect of major sell-offs to offset current losses in excess of £2bn. This is likely to include its agricultural holdings which will significantly impact on the Cooperative's model of responsible sourcing.

Future sources of capital for business raise broader questions about company futures. This is important for CSR given the prominence of publicly listed MNCs in the developments we have traced. One prospect is a growth of state-owned enterprises (SOEs), particularly resulting from the rise of China. These SOEs tend to reflect a state preference to maintain historic commitments to labour, which is consistent with some CSR expectations and an easy means of securing public finances, hardly a CSR end in itself. Unlike most Western counterparts, Chinese SOEs have an international significance as illustrated by the role of Chinese SOEs in Africa. They tend to be associated with significant contributions to African infrastructure development but also with CSR questions over the development of local labour forces and human rights. More recently Chinese SOEs have been buying Western companies, as evidenced by Bright Foods' majority shareholding in UK cereal maker Weetabix and the purchase of Australian food wholesaler, Manassen.

Another new business model has been piloted in the USA, known as 'Benefits' or 'B businesses'. These are designed to enable listed companies express an intention to combine a specified social benefit such as philanthropy or accountability with profit-making to which they would also be held accountable. Regulations have been approved in about a third of US states, including California, New York, and Delaware (the core state for US incorporation). It is as yet unclear how attractive this model will be or how B businesses will be differentiated from listed companies which maintain high CSR standards.

The relative status of publicly listed companies is unlikely to be seriously challenged in the immediate future. However, developments in sources of finance and in business models may mean that CSR will need to reflect different dynamics to those we have witnessed over the last few decades. It remains to be seen whether and how the socialization of markets will impact on SOEs and private equity, and how these companies will relate to the organizations of new governance and CSR.

Environmental and social futures

CSR will not simply reflect new economic and business circumstances but also their environmental and social context, and the way responsibilities are attached to the issues arising.

Climate change is one area for which companies, particularly in the energy and fossil-burning sectors, are often held responsible. Moreover, more companies are developing strategies in anticipation of climate change threats, both in particularly vulnerable regions, as well as in some sectors (e.g. insurance, civil engineering). Some companies specify climate change in their CSR policies, mainly related to systems for monitoring and reporting their carbon footprint, and technologies for minimizing this, often associated with cost-savings.

There are serious collective action problems which CSR companies are probably incapable of addressing without effective regulation of carbon impacts or the complete exhaustion of fossil fuels, which looks increasingly far off in the light of new extraction technologies. It is thus instructive that some oil companies in the USA and UK, and motor manufacturers in the RSA, have lobbied governments for more carbon emission regulations. Thus, in their power to influence regulators and consumers, as well as to innovate for reduced carbon impacts through new technologies such as electricity storage systems, hybrid and electric cars, corporations remain pivotal but not sufficient to address the climate change challenge.

The loss of ecological diversity is another, albeit less publicized, environmental risk. This is being integrated into some CSR thinking but very much at the margins, perhaps because many of the leading branded companies do not estimate their impacts here. These impacts are being publicized by NGOs, often around iconic species, such as the orang utan, rather than around systematic review of relevant business impacts.

Water depletion is another key environmental issue in some regions. Some leading companies like Coca Cola and Unilever are making headway in assessing their overall impacts on supply, and are building their policies on these insights. Others, like Walmart, focus on cost savings from more efficient use and re-use of water. Food security is emerging as a major challenge, reflecting combinations of urban migration, the attraction to farmers of non-food cash crops, and climate change, resulting in wheat and rice shortages, for example. Corporations are key actors in innovation and in the scaling up of innovation, including in food production and distribution.

Through the Millennium Development Goals (2000), UNGC corporations were enjoined to share the task of addressing the continuing problem of global wealth imbalances, particularly between sub-Saharan Africa and the rest of the world. The goals address: poverty and hunger; universal primary education; gender equality; child mortality; maternal health; HIV/AIDS, malaria, and other diseases; environmental sustainability; and global partnership for development. A post-2015 agenda has added commitments on women's and children's health, poverty, hunger, and disease.

Progress in addressing the poverty goal is probably mainly a function of economic growth in China, Brazil, and South-East

Asia. However, CSR schemes have also contributed to progress on other goals through 'bottom of the pyramid' schemes, the fair and ethical trade movements, and philanthropic efforts to address development issues. Issues of security, poverty, disease, education, governance, and capital flight remain critical to the lives of over a billion people. Corporations are hardly the only actors here, but their roles in wealth-creation, innovation, community relations, and governmental relations are all points of both criticism and opportunity.

More broadly yet, the context for some CSR agendas may change quite dramatically, as is illustrated in North Africa and the Middle East which have seen movements for liberalization, Jihadism, and returns to secular conservative authority in the space of a few years. In these circumstances the challenges for companies seeking to advance human rights and women's rights, in particular, are likely to be quite unpredictable.

CSR agendas

Economic and business, and environmental and social futures may well inform CSR agendas but companies retain discretion over their basic CSR commitments. There is no reason to expect recent company enthusiasm for membership of CSR organizations and the use of CSR standards to diminish. There are good reasons to see expansion of fair trade ranges and a widening of resource stewardship systems, for example. Other areas of growth are likely where companies identify clear business advantages from a CSR investment: thus gender and diversity policies to retain and attract labour in the context of skills shortages might be expected.

Some companies have complained about the plethora of reporting standards and other responsible business codes and their conflicting messages. It is therefore possible that some of these will fall into disuse and that others will be amalgamated. However, the institutionalization of CSR is at a very early stage and further standards and partnerships are also likely as new CSR agenda items emerge. There is every reason to expect that companies will continue to pursue these in multi-actor settings.

At a company level it is likely that there will be efforts to better manage CSR and this might be manifest in better integration of its disparate parts.

Integration is vital for companies to be confident about the pervasiveness of their CSR. Sustainability management makes sense only when sustainability accounting is integrated with mainstream management accounting. Anti-corruption policies only make sense when there is MNC-wide understanding of the company's ethical, risk, and regulatory commitments and systems. The responsibility of certain financial institutions will require trader awareness of their economic and social impacts, and ethical training and socialization, as anticipated in the UK's Lambert Report on Banking, 2014. It will also require CSR managers to understand and engage with, for example, financial derivatives.

CSR departments are likely to be strengthened through professionalization rather than through increased staff numbers. Their success in spreading CSR across corporations will depend less on their size than on their effectiveness in translating the CSR message across the firm, and in company leadership articulating the message. With this professionalization and integration, it could be expected that more companies will move from signing up to CSR initiatives and making community contributions. They can be expected to give more attention to transparency and that this will include fuller accounts of companies' environmental, social and governance impacts, rather than just the CSR outputs. A recent European study of CSR found that despite the overwhelming majority of companies perceiving CSR as important in general, and concurring more specifically with the importance of forty-seven out of forty-eight CSR issues posited, they had a much more limited understanding as to how to translate this awareness into activity. As a result, 'impact thinking' (e.g. how are communities effected by an activity?), as opposed to 'output thinking' (e.g. what company resources were spent on an activity?) was poorly developed. Companies therefore need to develop or acquire for tools and systems to evaluate CSR impacts so that they can take better account of the social and environmental impacts of their business operations in general, as well as of their CSR activities in particular.

CSR limitations

It could be countered that CSR is simply ephemeral in the context of the planet's problems because: first, most companies are not involved; secondly, many companies are only committed to CSR for 'ceremonial' reasons; and, thirdly, even the committed are more interested in CSR's impacts on their own business rather than the problems they are ostensibly addressing.

Although over 7,000 companies have signed the UN Global Compact and over 3,000 companies, including the world's largest 250, provide CSR reports, this remains a fraction of the world's companies. However, the world's largest 250 companies can have a significant impact on the social responsibility of business more widely through their up- and downstream effects. Moreover, thirty-five of the fifty (mainly financial) companies identified as 'the network of global control' have signed at least one of the UN Global Compact, the Extractive Industries Transparency Initiative, or the Equator Principles.

In the absence of wider transparency, it is by inference that we assume that the largest firms, and those with greatest economic control, inform the CSR of the remainder. Inference is supported by recent European research findings that small and medium-sized companies understand and value opportunities for responsible business even if they don't strategize or publicize this.

Furthermore, it could be objected that corporate signatures and rhetoric are hardly a reassuring basis for claims about the spread and effect of CSR. However, the rhetorical commitments of corporations appear to act as a soft form of regulation because companies tend not to welcome the accusation of hypocrisy if their CSR claims are found wanting. Instead they might, like Nike, invest in substantiating their CSR claims when criticized for not living up to them.

Finally, various studies of the impact of CSR on environmental and social problems have found little evidence of systematic efforts to identify, measure, and communicate impacts. This is likely to be an area where CSR will need to be strengthened. Too often companies are content to weigh and report their contributions in the form of finance or employee time; or company benefits, in terms of energy or water cost savings, or employee loyalty, for example. Whilst these data are clearly important for shareholders and senior managers, it is surely more widely important for companies to assess their impacts on a specified problem, be it reducing pollution, improving employment for marginalized workers, reducing poverty, or enhancing the health of consumers. There are problems of disentangling the effects of a single company's CSR from the impacts of other actors or trends, but nonetheless, if companies are able to isolate the impacts of single executives on profitability for the purposes of allocating bonuses, they are surely able to improve their accounts of CSR impact.

The social gaze

Throughout this *Very Short Introduction* we have seen that CSR critically depends on members of society being able to evaluate companies' behaviour, and being able to act thereon. This action can be through society members' roles as consumers, employees, and investors, or indirectly through their roles as citizens acting upon governments and civil society organizations.

The key developments we have observed, such as the expansion of CSR spheres from community to workplace, environment, and marketplace; the internationalization of CSR; the socialization of markets; and CSR in new governance all reinforce this interpretation. The arguments for CSR premised on the 'business case' rest on the assumption that the 'the social gaze' creates imperatives and rewards for responsible behaviour.

Although the 2007 financial crisis may have exhausted the patience of some people with the claims of, and hopes for CSR, it has certainly also re-energized societal attention to business responsibility. Most of the debate has been about options for more regulation on the assumption that business, particularly the banks, cannot otherwise be relied upon to behave responsibly.

Public opinion polls suggest that, if anything, general societal expectations of business continue to grow. Executive remuneration has been an easy target for the anti-corporates, the media, and politicians of all persuasions. Although Swiss voters rejected a 2014 referendum proposition to limit executive pay to twelve times the rate of the lowest paid (by 64 to 34 per cent) they had earlier supported a proposition which required greater shareholder controls over senior pay management packages. The financial sector is subject to policy debates about new regulations: for cross-border financial transactions; bank equity; and the composition of banks.

Whilst CSR-minded businesses may welcome some of these proposals, they do raise a general warning that business should also attend to restoring confidence in its trustworthiness. Business can contribute to the expansion of the social gaze through more encompassing CSR standards, and partnership networks offer just such an opportunity.

An elephant in the CSR room

Despite, first, the expansion of CSR to cover a very wide range of social, environmental, and governance issues, and secondly, the greater integration of CSR into wider societal governance, there appears to be something missing from CSR. There is very little said in CSR circles about *political* responsibility. For example, responsibility issues such as taxation, lobbying and political campaigning, and the special responsibilities of companies in monopolies and oligopolies for public goods and for critical infrastructure, are rarely referred to.

On the one hand this is a puzzle. Corporations in general have highly significant political impacts, through their (non-)payment of tax, their lobbying, and other kinds of engagement with politics, such as financing candidates and parties or recruiting former senior public officials and office-holders. Some companies also have market positions which have particular political salience by virtue of their, often monopolistic or oligopolistic, responsibility for distributing such public goods as energy and water. Others have responsibility for a variety of elements of critical infrastructure, notably information and communications systems, bank lending rates, international exchange systems. Only a few companies endeavour to manage these in the light of their CSR, or to devise their CSR to reflect these responsibilities. The socialization of market mechanisms and the new governance CSR organizations take little account of these.

Moreover, most environmental, social, and governance issues that CSR addresses have a very clear political character. They are concerned with activities that are consistent with conventional definitions of politics such as 'who gets what' and the 'authoritative allocation of values'. The socialization of markets reflects political processes in the form of citizen mobilization and in some cases, soft regulation by governments. The CSR organizations in new governance are partly populated by national and international governmental initiatives and organizations which align with and encourage CSR for public policy purposes.

On the other hand, perhaps this should not be puzzling, as corporations may be reticent to articulate their political engagements. They may expect greater criticism if they engage further in politics and, given that there are few frameworks to guide their behaviour here, they are aware of uncertainties about appropriate business engagement. During the 1980s, when CSR companies were doing great things to address the problem of unemployment, they apparently resisted entreaties from the UK Prime Minister, Margaret Thatcher, to get more involved in secondary education, precisely because they were uncertain as to how this would be publicly received.

Business may therefore consider that they will be damned if they do and damned if they don't frame their political activities in CSR terms. My own view, however, is that they will be more damned if they don't. Ambiguity and diffidence encourage cynicism. As noted above, business's wider roles are very much the subject of debate among public and politicians. All the more reason for companies and business associations to articulate their principles, develop frameworks, and identify and communicate their political impacts.

Prospects for corporate citizenship

In as much as business, civil society, and government do address the elephant in the CSR room by considering corporations' political roles more systemically, they are stressing the theme of 'corporate citizenship'.

Currently companies mainly describe their citizenship in terms of their community-level contributions and partnerships, the historical and conceptual core of CSR. In some cases, companies have extended this notion of citizenship as 'community activist' to 'political activist' by participating in boycotts of countries and governments (e.g. against the pre-revolution government in America, the apartheid South Africa, the Burmese military dictatorship). A number of companies, including Sam Adams and Heineken, withdrew sponsorship of the 2014 Boston and New York St Patrick's Day Parades in opposition to the decision to exclude lesbian, gay, bi-sexual and transgender organizations from participating in the parades. American Airlines, Apple, the Marriott hotel chain, and the Chamber of Commerce went even further and successfully petitioned the governor of Arizona to veto an anti-gay bill (SB1062) which had passed the state legislature. These cases illustrate that companies can take a view about public morality and act like human citizens to pursue these views.

More recently companies have taken this 'political activist' role a step further and have acted like citizens vis-à-vis other companies on social responsibility grounds. Following the revelations of phone hacking by employees of the UK paper, *News of the World*, many companies withdrew their advertising (e.g. Boots, Co-op, Ford, Halifax, Npower, O2, Sainsbury's, Specsavers, Vauxhall, Virgin Holidays). The Co-operative Group explained: 'These allegations have been met with revulsion by the vast majority of members who have contacted us.'

Secondly, corporations often take on neo-governmental roles. In some cases this reflects delegated powers to corporations for infrastructure, welfare, and education responsibilities in remote mining communities, for example. In other cases this reflects corporations assuming de facto regulatory powers by virtue of their market position. A good illustration is the Financial Coalition Against Child Pornography, a US organization of thirty-four leading banks, credit card companies, electronic payment networks, third-party payments companies, and internet services companies (including American Express, AOL, Google) dedicated to putting an end to commercial child pornography. Its activities overlap with those that one might expect of welfare, education, and crime detection agencies. UK banks have publicly warned ICT MNCs that unless the internet services guarantee that children are protected from violent and pornographic content, the systems for receiving payment from ICT users will be withdrawn, which would effectively shut down the internet services.

Some of the large corporations most committed to CSR extend their roles as broad societal change-agents. Unilever aims to use its business capacity to empower the marginalized; it has innovated in resource stewardship systems; and it has stimulated public debate over female body images. Novo Nordisk (diabetes) and GlaxoSmithKline (infant mortality) are systematically addressing major issues of disease and death. Significantly these cases of corporations taking on some of the really big challenges all involve CSR in new governance type relationships. But these contributions and the processes that underpin them are not accounted for in political terms.

Thirdly, the ICT corporations facilitate the political roles of their own stakeholders and human citizens more widely. The models of fair trade, SRI and ETI precisely reflect this ability of the corporation to enable consumers, investors, and organized labour to pursue their agendas of international development, climate change, and trade union recognition, for example.

New media, like the E.ON YouTube channel and the BP Energy Lab, enable corporations to facilitate wider citizenship participation through the corporate arenas of debate that they create themselves. More generally, social media provided by ICT companies enable individual citizenship agendas to be more effectively pursued than do other channels of participation. One example is of a Chinese citizen and media personality, Rui Chenggang, who successfully challenged Starbuck's location in the Forbidden City. Whilst he had failed to raise the salience of the issue through traditional media, his new media campaign soon attracted a petition of 500,000 signatures and his blog posting was soon picked up by the traditional media.

So there is an elephant in the CSR room: the political roles of corporations are usually excluded from their own accounts of CSR. Yet companies are well able to engage like human citizens, to take neo-governmental roles, and to facilitate the citizenship of others. When human beings adopt and combine these political roles, they are usually described as citizens and their activities as citizenship. So why don't corporations think and talk more in citizenship terms?

A reasonable retort to this challenge would be to ask what might be entailed in 'corporate citizenship' as a considered way of managing political responsibilities (rather than as another name for CSR)? If the model of CSR development over the last two decades is a guide, then a blend of self, social, and soft governmental regulation looks propitious. For example, companies could include details and explanations of their taxation returns and their lobbying and campaigning activities in their ESG reports. Business associations, civil society, and appropriate professionals could develop frameworks to agree principles with which to guide companies in reporting and managing these responsibilities. Existing CSR organizations and standards could be expanded to include these criteria. Governments could also improve their own transparency systems in terms of how corporate tax regulations are applied, and the details of how they are lobbied.

But as with CSR more generally, this is not about adding rules for their own sake. The longer term intention is that citizenly habits of being ruled, sharing in ruling and facilitating the participation of others are instilled in business–society relations. These issues will need to be thought through, debated, principles agreed, built into company and CSR systems, business education, and professional development. If this seems far-fetched, one can reflect on how, twenty years ago, one might have viewed the developments which inform CSR today…a little far-fetched?

With reference to Adam Smith's quote at the outset of this *Very Short Introduction*, the public good afforded by CSR is not simply a function of those who 'affect to trade' to that end, though companies remain the key actors. It is also a joint enterprise such that those who trade are encouraged (by the socialization of markets) and enjoined (through CSR and new governance systems) to do so according to society's conceptions of responsibility. Whereas Arrow had anticipated non-market institutions bridging a market–society gap, we are witnessing market and non-market institutions collaborating in bridging that gap. That is what makes CSR so interesting and why it does have potential to enable companies, in Adam Smith's terms, to 'trade for the public good'.

References

Chapter 1: An idea whose time has come

A. B. Carroll, 'A three dimensional model of corporate social performance', *Academy of Management Review* 4:4 (1979).

K. Davis, 'The case for and against business assumption of social responsibility', *Academy of Management Journal* 16:2 (1973).

D. Matten and J. Moon '"Implicit" and "Explicit" CSR: A conceptual framework for a comparative understanding of corporate social responsibility', *Academy of Management Review* 33:2 (2008).

M. Moody-Stuart, *Responsible Leadership: Lessons from the Front Line of Sustainability and Ethics* (Greenleaf, 2014).

Chapter 2: The company level

A. B. Carroll, 'A three dimensional model of corporate social performance', *Academy of Management Review* 4:4 (1979). The pyramid is reproduced in A. K. Buchholtz and A. B. Carroll, *Business and Society* (Southwestern, 8th edn, 2011).

J. Elkington, *Cannibals with Forks: the Triple Bottom Line of 21st Century Business* (Capstone, 1997).

R. E. Freeman, *Strategic Management: A Stakeholder Perspective* (Pitman, 1984; re-published in a print-on-demand edn by Cambridge, 2010). Ed Freeman has reworked the model, e.g. R. E. Freeman, J. S. Harrison, and A. C. Wicks (eds), *Managing for Stakeholders* (Yale, 2007).

M. E. Porter and M. R. Kramer, 'Creating shared value', *Harvard Business Review* January–February (2011). See also <http://sharedvalue.org/about-shared-value>.

Chapter 3: National and international developments

M. Gjølberg, 'Measuring the immeasurable? Constructing an index of CSR practices and CSR performance in 20 countries', *Scandinavian Journal of Management* 25:1 (2009).

D. Matten and J. Moon, '"Implicit" and "Explicit" CSR', *Academy of Management Review* 33:2 (2008).

Chapter 6: Critical perspectives

J. Bakan, *The Corporation: The Pathological Pursuit of Profit and Power* (Robinson Publishing, 2005).

A. Berle and G. Means *The Modern Corporation and Private Property* (Harcourt, Brace and World, 1932).

P. Fleming and M. V. Jones, *The End of Corporate Social Responsibility: Crisis and Critique* (Sage, 2012).

M. Friedman, 'The social responsibility of business is to increase its profits', *New York Times Magazine* (13 September 1970).

F. Guerrera, 'Welch rues short-term profit "obsession"', *Financial Times* (12 March 2009).

M. C. Jensen and R. S. Meckling, 'Theory of the firm: Managerial behavior, agency costs and ownership structure', *Journal of Financial Economics* 3:4 (1976).

R. Reich, *Beyond Outrage: What Has Gone Wrong with our Economy and our Democracy and How to Fix It* (Vintage, 2012).

Chapter 7: Prospects and reflections

S. Vitali, J. B. Glattfelder, and S. Battiston, 'The network of global control' (open-access article distributed under the terms of the Creative Commons Attribution License, 2012).

Further reading

General

Although ethical, polemical, and manifesto writing about the responsibilities of people in business and of businesses is very long-standing, CSR is a relative newcomer as an academic field. Question of responsibility and power of the modern corporation emerged as a corporate governance theme regarding such questions as 'To whom are corporate managers responsible?' and 'How can corporate power be accounted for and regulated?' The first systematic analysis of CSR is usually credited to H. R. Bowen's *Social Responsibilities of the Businessman* (Harper & Row, 1953).

Today CSR is a thriving scholarly field with articles in journals of management and business, organizations studies, accounting and accountability, business ethics and corporate governance, and business and society. There is also a lively practitioner-oriented literature.

There are numerous CSR textbooks, handbooks, and readers, e.g.:

M. Blowfield and A. Murray, *Corporate Responsibility: A Critical Reader* (Oxford University Press, 2008).

A. K. Buchholtz and A. B. Carroll, *Business and Society: Ethics, Sustainability, and Stakeholder Management* (Southwestern, 8th edn, 2011).

A. Crane, D. Matten, and L.J. Spence (eds), *Corporate Social Responsibility: Readings and Cases in Global Context* (Routledge 2nd edn, 2014).

A. Crane, A. McWilliams, D. Matten, J. Moon, and D. Siegel (eds), *The Oxford Handbook of Corporate Social Responsibility* (Oxford University Press, 2008).

C. Crouch and C. MacLean (eds), *The Responsible Corporation in a Global Economy* (Oxford University Press, 2011).

J.-P. Gond and J. Moon (eds), *Corporate Social Responsibility: A Reader* (Routledge, 4 vols, 2012).

D. Matten and J. Moon (eds), *Corporate Citizenship: A Reader* (Edward Elgar, 2013).

A. G. Scherer and G. Palazzo (eds), *Handbook of Research on Global Corporate Citizenship* (Edward Elgar, 2008).

N. C. Smith, C. B. Bhattacharya, D. Vogel, and D. I. Levine (eds), *Global Challenges in Responsible Business* (Cambridge University Press, 2010).

D. L. Swanson and M. Orlitzky, *Toward Integrative Corporate Citizenship: Research Advances in Corporate Social Performance* (Palgrave, 2008).

There are several websites which provide a variety of documents on and analysis of CSR, e.g.:

International Centre for Corporate Social Responsibility <http://www.nottingham.ac.uk/business/ICCSR>.

Copenhagen Business School CSR <http://www.cbs.dk/en/research/departments-and-centres/ department-of-intercultural-communication-and-management/ centre-corporate-social-responsibility>.

Boston College Corporate Citizenship Centre <http://www.bcccc.net>.

Chapter 1: An idea whose time has come

Further discussion of CSR definitions and evolution: J.-P. Gond and J. Moon, 'Corporate social responsibility in retrospect and prospect: Exploring the life-cycle of an essentially contested concept', in Gond and Moon (eds), *Corporate Social Responsibility: A Reader* (Routledge, 2012; reprinted at <http://www.nottingham.ac.uk/business/ICCSR/research. php?action=single&id=78>).

Recent CSR developments: see websites of CSR media (Box 3), CSR organizations (Box 14). CSR consultants provide easily accessible CSR updates, e.g.: <http://www.goodcorporation.com>, <http://corporate-citizenship.com>.

CSR leadership: D. Swanson, 'Top managers as drivers for Corporate Social Responsibility', in A. Crane et al. (eds), *The Oxford*

Handbook of Corporate Social Responsibility (Oxford University Press, 2008).

The 'social gaze' is adapted from: J. Boswell, 'The informal social control of business in Britain: 1880–1939', *The Business History Review* 57:2 (1983).

The shift from corporate-centred to corporate-oriented CSR is explored in: A. Rasche, F. G. A. de Bakker, and J. Moon, 'Complete and partial organizing for corporate social responsibility', *Journal of Business Ethics* 115:4 (2014).

Chapter 2: The company level

Recommended papers for CSR in the four spheres are as follows.

Community: D. Hess, N. Rogovsky and T. W. Dunphy, 'The next wave of corporate community involvement', *California Management Review* 37:4 (2002).

Workplace: J.-P. Gond, A. El Akremi, J. Igalens, and V. Swaen, 'A corporate social responsibility–corporate financial performance behavioural model for employees', in Smith et al. (eds), *Global Challenges in Responsible Business* (Cambridge University Press, 2010).

Marketplace: (upstream) S. J. Frenkel and D. Scott, 'Compliance, collaboration and codes of labor practice', *California Management Review* 45:1 (2002); (downstream) R. Caruana and A. Crane, 'Constructing Consumer Responsibility', *Organization Studies* 29:12 (2008).

Environment: S. L. Hart, 'Beyond greening: Strategies for a sustainable world', *Harvard Business Review*, January–February (1997).

Organization and integration: P. Mirvis and B. Googins, 'Stages of corporate citizenship', *California Management Review* 48:2 (2006); K. Bondy, J. Moon, and D. Matten, 'An institution of corporate social responsibility (CSR) in multi-national corporations (MNCs)', *Journal of Business Ethics* 111:2 (2012).

CSR performance and impact: J. D. Margolis and J. P. Walsh, 'Misery loves companies: Rethinking social initiatives by business', *Administrative Science Quarterly* 48:2 (2003); <http://www.csr-impact.eu>.

Chapter 3: National and international developments

USA: A. B. Carroll, 'Corporate social responsibility: Evolution of a definitional construct', *Business and Society* 38:3 (1999).

UK: J. Moon 'UK—An explicit model of business–society relations', in
A. Habisch, J. Jonker, M. Wegner, and R. Schmidpeter (eds),
Corporate Social Responsibility Across Europe (Springer, 2005).

International: W. Visser and N. Tolhurst (eds), *The World Guide to
CSR: A Country-by-Country Analysis of Corporate Sustainability
and Responsibility* (Greenleaf, 2010); W. Chapple and J. Moon,
'CSR in Asia', *Business and Society* 44:4 (2005); P. Dobers and M.
Halme, 'Corporate social responsibility and developing countries',
CSR and Environmental Management 16:5 (2009); D. Jamali, Y.
Sidani, and K. El-Asmar, 'A three country comparative analysis of
managerial CSR perspectives: Insights from Lebanon, Syria and
Jordan', *Journal of Business Ethics* 85:2 (2009); V. M. Strike, J. Gao,
and P. Bansal, 'Being good while being bad: Social responsibility and
the international diversification of US firms', *Journal of
International Business Studies* 37:6 (2006); J. G. Ruggie,
'Reconstituting the global public domain issues, actors and
practices', *European Journal of International Relations* 10:4 (2004).

Chapter 4: The socialization of markets

General: D. Vogel, *The Market for Virtue: The Potential and Limits of
Corporate Social Responsibility* (Brooking Institution Press, 2005).

Market factors: C. B. Bhattacharya and S. Sen, 'Doing better at doing
good: When, why and how consumers respond to corporate social
initiatives', *California Management Review* 47:1 (2004); P. Rivoli
'Making a difference or making a statement? Finance research and
socially responsible investment', *Business Ethics Quarterly* 13:3
(2003); C. B. Bhattacharya, S. Sen, and D. Korschun, 'Using
corporate social responsibility to win the war for talent', *MIT Sloan
Management Review* 49:2 (2008).

Social Factors: R. V. Aguilera, D. E. Rupp, C. A. Williams, and
J. Ganapathi, 'Putting the S back in corporate social responsibility',
Academy of Management Review 32:3 (2008); F. Den Hond and
F. G. D. De Bakker, 'Ideologically motivated activism: How activist
groups influence corporate social change activities', *Academy of
Management Review* 32:3 (2007).

Governmental factors: J. S. Knudsen, J. Moon, and R. Slager,
'Government policies for corporate social responsibility in Europe',
Policy and Politics forthcoming (2014); J.-P. Gond, N. Kang, and
J. Moon, 'The government of self-regulation', *Economy and Society*
40:4 (2011).

Chapter 5: CSR and new governance

J. Moon, 'Business social responsibility and new governance', *Government and Opposition* 37:3 (2002).

A. Scherer, G. Palazzo, and D. Baumann, 'Global rules and private actors: Towards a new role of the transnational corporation in global governance', *Business Ethics Quarterly* 16:4 (2006).

D. U. Gilbert, A. Rasche, and S. A. Waddock, 'Accountability in a global economy: The emergence of international accountability standards', *Business Ethics Quarterly* 21:1 (2011).

Chapter 6: Critical perspectives

L. Stout, *The Shareholder Value Myth: How Putting Shareholders First Harms Investors, Corporations, and the Public* (Berrett–Koehler, 2012).

R. Shamir, 'Mind the gap: The commodification of Corporate Social Responsibility', *Symbolic Interaction* 28:2 (2005).

On essentially contested concepts see: W. B. Gallie 'Essentially contested concepts', *Proceedings of the Aristotelian Society* 56:1 (1955–6).

Chapter 7: Prospects and reflections

Corporate citizenship is explored in: J. Moon, A. Crane, and D. Matten, 'Can corporations be citizens: Corporate citizenship as a metaphor for business participation in society', *Business Ethics Quarterly* 15:3 (2004); A. Crane, D. Matten, and J. Moon, *Corporations and Citizenship* (Cambridge University Press, 2008); and D. Matten and J. Moon, 'Corporate citizenship: Introducing business as an actor in political governance', in D. Matten and J. Moon (eds), *Corporate Citizenship A Reader* (Edward Elgar, 2013; reprinted in <http://www.nottingham.ac.uk/business/ICCSR/research.php?action=single&id=83>).

Index

C

SOCIAL MEDIA
Very Short Introduction

Join our community

www.oup.com/vsi

- Join us online at the official Very Short Introductions
  Facebook page.
- Access the thoughts and musings of our authors with our
  online **blog**.
- Sign up for our monthly **e-newsletter** to receive information
  on all new titles publishing that month.
- Browse the full range of Very Short Introductions online.
- Read **extracts** from the Introductions for free.
- Visit our library of **Reading Guides**. These guides, written by our
  expert authors will help you to question again, why you think
  what you think.
- If you are a teacher or lecturer you can order inspection
  copies quickly and simply via our website.

ONLINE CATALOGUE
A Very Short Introduction

Our online catalogue is designed to make it easy to find your ideal Very Short Introduction. View the entire collection by subject area, watch author videos, read sample chapters, and download reading guides.